MAKE YOUR BED FIRST

EASY TOOLS FOR TEENS TO SUCCEED IN LIFE

THE ESSENTIAL GUIDE TO ADOPT GOOD HABITS

GILL GRANT

ABOUT THE AUTHOR

Allow me to introduce myself—I'm Gill Grant, a self-taught explorer of the human mind, and I'm on a mission to make a difference as a compassionate global traveler. At 52 years young, I believe in boundless energy and a deep well of empathy, qualities that have fueled my incredible journey.

While I spent many years studying psychology in traditional academic settings, I came to realize that genuine understanding doesn't solely come from books and lectures. It blossoms from immersing oneself in the diverse tapestry of human experiences across the world. This realization inspired me to embark on a unique path of self-discovery.

My travels have taken me from the bustling streets of New Delhi to the serene villages of Africa. In each place, I've rolled up my sleeves and worked alongside communities facing a multitude of challenges. Through my humanitarian missions, I've touched countless lives, leaving behind an indelible mark of empathy and support.

As a tireless advocate for personal growth and mental well-being, I transitioned from the academic world to a hands-on approach. My psychology background enables me to connect with individuals from all walks of life, providing me with profound insights into the complexities of the human psyche.

My approach to self-help is not just about offering advice; it's about fostering genuine connections and equipping individuals with the tools to navigate life's challenges with resilience and self-compassion. My warm and relatable style has resonated with people worldwide, transcending cultural boundaries.

I invite you to join me on this journey of self-help discovery, where every page is an invitation to embrace personal growth, mental well-being, and the boundless capacity of the human spirit. My message is clear: You have the power to transform your life, and I'm here as your guide, mentor, and friend on this incredible journey.

HERE IS A FREE GIFT FOR YOU!

Scan the code below to get your free copy of
"5 KEY ATTITUDES for SUCCESS"

Let me introduce my guidebook for teens, parents and teachers too

…to inspire our children to <u>become the best version of themselves.</u>

<u>Just scan the QR code below:</u>

CONTENTS

INTRODUCTION

It's not easy being a teenager, and while you have your dreams and aspirations, you may wonder if you'll ever be able to achieve them. If we're feeling negative about our chances for success, it may seem like a lot of hard work with no guarantee of success.

However, we all have the potential to change our lives and lead a more meaningful existence.

You don't have to wait until adulthood if you want to transform your life to reach specific goals. If you start working now, you can become the best version of yourself even sooner. You can do all this by starting useful daily habits and sticking to them. It's about the significance of morning routines, and it all starts with making your bed.

Let's set the scene. Have you ever felt that you should be doing and achieving more but something is holding you back? Maybe you feel frustrated that you're not fulfilling your potential or that there's a better version of yourself that you can't quite seem to become yet. Don't worry, you're not alone with these uncertainties. Most of us want to lead more productive and purposeful lives.

We're going to take a transformative journey to find the strength and resilience in ourselves, through the power of habit, to unlock your hidden potential.

You may have doubts and, at times, feel as if you're stagnating on your personal growth journey. This book will give you the motivation to continue and overcome the doubts that may be preventing you from reaching self-awareness. It will be your companion and guide on the way to achieving a more satisfying and meaningful life.

This book will also show you that through a simple morning routine, such as making your bed, you can set out on your self-development journey of becoming the best version of yourself.

We'll guide you through the art of habit formation and personal development, helping you unlock your potential along the way. We're committed to providing you with the insights, strategies, and real-world examples you need to succeed.

KEY TAKEAWAYS

Let's explore some of the key takeaways:

Chapter 1—Positive Habits

This chapter looks at the importance of seemingly small habits, like making your bed. By instilling positive rituals in our daily lives, we create habits that become the building blocks of discipline, setting the tone for a day filled with intention and accomplishment.

Chapter 2—Decluttering Your Mind

It's important to declutter your mind for the sake of a focused and meaningful life. Through practical strategies, readers learn to navigate the labyrinth of thoughts, fostering mental resilience and tranquility.

Chapter 3—Ownership and Self-Care

Ownership of one's life and the practice of self-care are the main themes of this chapter. Taking responsibility for our well-being becomes an act of self-love.

Chapter 4—Healthy Environment

Our surroundings significantly impact our well-being. This chapter looks at the importance of fostering a healthy environment. From the spaces we inhabit to the relationships we nurture, creating a positive ecosystem lays the groundwork for a thriving and balanced life.

Chapter 5 — Visual Order and Your Room

Visual order extends beyond aesthetics; it also forms our mental landscape. From the arrangement of our living spaces to the simplicity of a clutter-free room, you'll learn how to harness the power of visual harmony for enhanced focus and tranquility.

Chapter 6 — Psychological Comfort

This chapter takes a look at how good habits can create psychological comfort.

Chapter 7 — Personal Pride

Personal pride becomes a driving force in this chapter. Understanding the value of your accomplishments can help you foster a sense of pride and build your self-esteem and a belief in your abilities.

Chapter 8 — Emotional Intelligence, Emotional Regulation, and Positive Habits

This chapter equips you with the tools to navigate the complex landscape of emotions. Understanding and managing your feelings is vital for building healthy relationships and fostering resilience. If you have these skills, you'll be able to deal with most things life throws your way.

Chapter 9—Failure, Success, Procrastination, and a Growth Mindset

We look at how failure can teach you valuable lessons on the road to success and how you can develop a growth mindset.

Chapter 10—Critical Thinking Skills

Critical thinking is your ability to analyze information, understand the logical connections between ideas, and make informed decisions. This chapter considers why it's so important to have these essential skills and also the role they play in society.

So, are you ready to start your self-improvement journey by taking small steps such as making your bed? Let's get started with the simple stuff before we move on to the more serious topics like emotional intelligence and critical thinking.

CHAPTER 1
POSITIVE HABITS

❝ *Good habits formed in youth make all the difference.*

ARISTOTLE

Alex couldn't see the point of making his bed every morning. His parents, who were neat freaks, had always insisted on this daily chore ever since he could remember. They would remind him every morning to make his bed, while he would roll his eyes at them. They told him that it was all about the discipline. He couldn't care less, though. In his world, Fortnite victories and basketball dunks were what mattered.

Then, one day at school, the basketball coach told Alex's team that they would do discipline training and that they all needed to start by making their beds every morning. Alex couldn't believe what he was hearing.

"Why do we need to do that, Coach?" he blurted out.

The coach smiled and told him that it was all about developing a winning mindset.

Alex was surprised and intrigued. He decided to give it a try. The next morning, he thought about what his coach had said.

He realized that making his bed had made him feel a sense of accomplishment. He started his day by achieving something, even if it was something small. Getting busy and moving around made him motivated to do more and to start his day with a renewed sense of energy.

He also felt confident and ready to take on other challenges. His neat room gave him a sense of clarity, and he realized that when he made his bed, he showed respect for his space. He treated his room with care and respect, similar to how he treated his gaming setup.

Alex had a long and exhausting game, but he immediately felt better when he returned home after practice to his bed that had already been made. It felt as if he had entered a stress-free zone and like his bedroom was his haven.

Alex then realized that making his bed wasn't just about a tidy room. It was about the mental and emotional boost it gave him—the mindset of a winner.

From that day onward, Alex became a bed-making champion. His grades improved, he achieved higher scores in basketball, and he even saw improvements in his online gaming skills. Alex had managed to unlock the power of a winning mindset, and it had all started with a simple task: making his bed.

STARTING YOUR DAY WITH A SMALL WIN

Maybe you're like Alex and beginning your day by making your bed may seem like a simple, unimportant task.

This may not seem exciting for a teenager with more important things on their mind, but getting into this simple habit can fill you with a sense of accomplishment and set a positive tone for everything that will happen to you the rest of your day.

Making your bed is more than just a chore—it's a small win waiting to happen. Here's how this small task can inspire you:

- When you make your bed in the morning, it's your first success or goal for the day. That feeling of accomplishment is a powerful motivator. It's similar to the rush you get when you complete a tough level in your favorite video game or you win at a sports game. By making your bed, you start your day with a win, and that's a fantastic way to boost your confidence.
- Making your bed every day—first thing in the morning—also sets the stage for a structured morning routine. Think of it as the foundation of a daily schedule that brings stability to your life. It provides you with the rules you can follow for the rest of your day.
- Small actions, like making your bed, can be a stepping stone for forming other good habits. As you experience the benefits of consistency, you might be inspired to adopt more healthy routines.

BUILDING HABITS

It can take a while to build positive habits, and it's an ongoing process. However, you'll lead a happier and more successful life if you're able to make positive changes in your life constantly. One of the ways of doing this is through habit stacking.

What Is Habit Stacking?

The term "habit stacking" was popularized by James Clear, author of the best-selling book *Atomic Habits*. While he didn't necessarily coin the term, he introduced and explained the concept of habit stacking in his book. Habit stacking involves integrating a new habit into your existing routine by "stacking" it on top of a habit you already perform consistently. This technique makes it easier to remember to do the new habit by associating it with an established one.

A practical way to explain it is to look at what happens when we learn a new language.

For example, you're learning German as a foreign language. The class starts with an exciting introduction to a new topic. Your brain is now fired up, and you're ready to learn more.

Then, you move to the next part of your class, where you learn new words and phrases in German. You might even complete activities with a partner.

New information and skills don't just get dumped on you all at the same time. The teacher might even give you a short quiz before moving on to the main part of the lesson.

After the hard work, there's a cooldown period where the teacher will sum up what you've learned.

Habit stacking is about taking small steps to learn and grow. Eventually, you put the small habits together that you've learned when you're on the way to achieving your big goals. It's difficult to change your behavior in a positive way, but habit stacking can help you with this process.

Habit stacking is based on the idea that we want routine in our lives, and we tend to act according to this. So, with habit stacking, you build on the routines you already have. For example, if you want to keep to your new habit of making your bed every day, make sure you do it in the same sequence of actions. You wake up, get dressed, and then make your bed.

What happens is that you become neurologically wired to do things in a certain sequence. Your brain is already used to doing certain things on autopilot in the morning, such as taking a shower before getting dressed and then brushing your teeth. Making your bed simply becomes another step in your routine. Your brain doesn't have to build entirely new synaptic connections if you add making your bed to your routine.

You can try habit stacking in the following way:

1. Start by observing how your typical day goes. Take notes on what's happening around you and how you spend your time. You can write down in your journal what you do every hour or use some of your digital devices.

2. Pay attention to the habits you already have. These are the things you do at about the same time every day, like getting ready for school or having your meals. Hopefully, making your bed will soon be one of them!

3. Choose a new habit, such as making your bed, that you want to add to your routine. Be clear about what it is and when you're going to do it. For example, if your goal is to take a 15-minute break to go for a walk, specify when and where you'll do it. Maybe you'll walk around in your garden after school.

4. Now, you'll have to think about which of your current habits is the best match for your

new goal. For instance, if you want to start making your bed, will you do it before or after you brush your teeth? Or, will you be more likely to do it after you get dressed?

5. Commit to trying this new habit stack for a week. Did you stick with the routine? Did it make you feel good? Don't worry if you missed a day, just try again.

Creating Lasting Habits

Your habits are rooted in how you see yourself, so if you want to build positive new habits, you have to reshape your identity and cause a shift in how you perceive yourself.

People often pursue outcomes and results without first taking a look at their identity. The trick is understanding yourself and your outlook on the world, including how you judge yourself and others.

Consider the type of person you really want to be and the type of adjustments you would need to make to achieve this desired identity. You should start with small habit changes, which will eventually help you achieve your main goal.

For example, you decide you want to complete a novel that you're writing within the year. This is an ambitious goal, and you're more likely to achieve it if you break it up into smaller goals. So, start by building the habit of writing a few paragraphs every day. If this habit aligns with your chosen identity, it will be the foundation for your long-term habits that will lead to positive results.

The main idea behind this approach is to evolve into the person you want to become. When you have ingrained, identity-based habits, you'll be much less reliant on motivation only to achieve your objectives.

Planning Your Actions

Mia was an ambitious teenager with big dreams who wasn't quite sure how to turn her dreams into reality.

Her dream was to become an artist. She had a deep passion for painting, and her room was full of paint-brushes and canvases. She felt like creating beautiful artwork most days, but somehow, she couldn't seem to turn her motivation into action.

One day, as she sat daydreaming, she realized wishing for success wasn't enough. She actually needed a plan She needed to get some discipline and useful habits in her life to bridge the gap between what she wanted and the actions she was failing to take.

Mia has never been good at writing things down, but she made a rough plan in her head of what she was going to do. She sat her easel up by her window and positioned her paint and brushes beside it. She decided she would paint every morning after waking up because that was when she could get the best natural light.

By following her new habit every morning, Mia's artistic journey started to transform, and she saw significant improvement in her work.

She didn't wait for motivation and inspiration any longer. Instead, she would get up every morning and head straight for her easel and paintbrushes.

The consistent practice made all the difference to her work, and her dream to be an artist was no longer a distant dream.

So, like Mia, you don't have to rely only on motivation to help you get ahead in life. If you have a plan and the right habits, these will trigger your actions.

MOTIVATION AND HABITS

Let's talk about motivation. That's almost like a magical force that gets you up and going in life, even when you don't feel like doing things. It inspires you to take all kinds of actions—from the simple ones like eating when you're hungry to big life decisions like deciding what you want to study one day.

You get different types of motivation, and one popular theory is Maslow's hierarchy of needs. Picture it like a pyramid, starting with basic needs at the bottom, like air and water, and climbing up to more complex ones, such as the need for love and self-actualization—reaching your full potential.

Maslow's theory suggests that you need to fulfill your basic needs first before focusing on higher-level ones. For instance, you need food and shelter before diving into personal development and fulfilling your potential.

Then, there's the incentive theory, which says people do things for rewards. Think of it as extrinsic (external) and intrinsic (internal) motivation. Extrinsic is like doing a task for a reward or to avoid punishment, while intrinsic is doing something because you find it rewarding in itself.

Intrinsic motivation, the internal drive, is deeply rooted in your identity and can be a long-lasting source of motivation. Unlike external rewards, it gives you genuine satisfaction.

Now, how do you boost intrinsic motivation? First off, you need to improve your self-confidence—the belief that you can achieve something. If you think you can, you're more likely to get through setbacks.

Have you ever thought about volunteering? It's a fantastic way to boost intrinsic motivation and give back. Helping others without expecting anything in return is a surefire way to feel internally motivated.

Your motivation should be tied to a purpose that's important to you. You need to understand what drives you and how your daily activities contribute to a bigger purpose.

A good way to get motivated is not to wait until you feel like doing things. Sometimes, starting an activity will get you into the rhythm, and your internal motivation will kick in. Setting routines and challenging yourself with achievable goals also works wonders.

Cultivate a love of learning. Stay curious, ask questions, and don't fear failure. Learning about yourself will increase your intrinsic motivation. You need to develop a lifelong learning mentality, which will encourage you to learn throughout your life.

Live a purposeful life. Chase goals that truly matter to you, not what others think you should pursue.

Hold yourself accountable for achieving your personal goals.

Good habits will trigger motivation and can even help you start something new. Successful people have habits based on their values, focus on positive progress, and are always learning.

INTRINSIC MOTIVATION

So, why is intrinsic motivation the force you really need to get ahead in life?

In simple terms, intrinsic motivation is the inner drive that pushes you to do something because you find it rewarding in itself, not for external rewards like money or praise. It's that feeling you get when you're passionate about a hobby, like playing an instrument, writing, or drawing, just because it brings you joy.

When you're intrinsically motivated to do something, you can often work at it for hours on end until you completely lose track of time.

Now, imagine you're tackling a challenging video game. You don't do it for a prize; you do it because you love the thrill of overcoming obstacles and conquering levels. That's intrinsic motivation at play!

Intrinsic motivation gives you genuine satisfaction and fulfillment. When you take part in activities you love doing—for example, creative activities such as painting or even any type of sport—you will get a sense of accomplishment from within, and that makes your experience even more meaningful.

Unlike external rewards, which can be fleeting, intrinsic motivation is like a long-lasting fuel source. It's a continuous source of energy that keeps you going, even when you have to deal with challenges.

Intrinsic motivation is deeply personal. It's about doing things that align with your values, interests, and passions. This personal connection makes the journey more enjoyable and purposeful.

When you're intrinsically motivated, setbacks become stepping stones. You're more likely to bounce back from challenges, learn from failures, and keep moving forward with resilience.

Intrinsic motivation and learning go hand in hand. When you're curious and eager to explore new things, you're more likely to absorb knowledge effortlessly and make your learning experience more enjoyable.

How can you boost your intrinsic motivation?

First, believe in yourself! Enhance your self-efficacy, which is the belief that you can achieve tasks. This positive mindset will boost your determination and perseverance.

Stay curious and question things around you. Be open to learning, even if it means stepping out of your comfort zone. The more you learn, the better you understand yourself.

Take part in activities you're passionate about. Whether it's playing a sport, creating art, or exploring new subjects, pursuing your passions fuels intrinsic motivation.

Connect your daily activities to bigger purposes. Understand how each small step contributes to your larger goals, as this sense of purpose can enhance your motivation.

GOAL-SETTING

Setting goals isn't just some fancy advice for adults; it's like having a game plan for your future. Imagine it as your guide to leveling up in everything you do, from school projects and your favorite hobbies to deciding what kind of career you want in the future. This isn't about impressing anyone else; it's about pushing yourself ahead in life.

Reasons for Setting Goals

Imagine you're on a road trip without a destination. Setting goals gives you direction and focus in life. Whether doing well in a test or winning a sports game, setting goals will guide you on your way to achieving success.

Have you ever felt pumped up after achieving something, even if it's small? It gives you a reason to get out of bed, tackle challenges, and celebrate your victories. Every goal you achieve will give you a confidence boost.

When you have clear goals, you also become better at managing your time, as you know what you need to achieve and by when. This will help you get things done more efficiently, and you can say goodbye to procrastination.

Goals allow you to dream big and then break those dreams into achievable steps. Whether you dream of becoming a doctor, artist, or pro athlete, goals can help you turn your dreams into reality.

Life can throw curveballs at you and give you a plan to overcome obstacles, learn from setbacks, and keep moving forward. Challenges become stepping stones instead of roadblocks.

Setting goals also lets you explore different areas. You could even discover a talent or passion you never knew you had before. It's a journey of discovering your own self-awareness.

Goals aren't just for now; they're building blocks for your future. Whether it's about completing your studies and landing a good job, starting a business, or traveling the world, setting goals is shaping the foundation for the fantastic life you want to lead.

Different Goal-Setting Techniques

Many different techniques will make it easier for you to set your goals. Let's look at a summary of some of the main techniques.

SMART Goals

You may have heard of this technique, and it has been discussed in many different publications.

It stands for the following:

- Specific: Your goal needs to be clear. For example, if you want to create a website, create a clear plan of what you want to include on your site.
- Measurable: You should be able to measure your goals and milestones. For example, do

you want to achieve a certain number of views for your website at a certain time?

- Achievable: Will your goals fit in with your current lifestyle? For example, if you want to start a business, would you be able to do this along with your school work?
- Relevant: Your goals should be meaningful and need to align with your overall objectives. The goal makes sense in the broader context of your personal and professional aspirations.
- Time-bound: Set timelines for yourself. When do you want your business to be up and running?

HARD Technique

This stands for making your goals heartfelt, animated, required, and difficult:

- Your goals should be connected to your emotions, and you should be able to visualize your success by feeling, smelling, and tasting it.
- Your goals should also link to something you're required to do. It becomes more meaningful, for example, if you can link them to a school project.

- You should challenge yourself by setting difficult goals, but they should still be achievable. Your goals should make you feel accomplished when you achieve them.

WOOP Goals

This type of goal-setting works particularly well if you need to break some bad habits. WOOP stands for the following:

- Wish: Wish for an exciting goal and feel positive about it.
- Outcome: Visualize success vividly and feel how happy you will be when you achieve it.
- Obstacle: Identify potential obstacles and think about how you will overcome them.
- Plan: Work on solutions. Connect with someone who can guide you.

Micro Goals

Divide your big goals into smaller, achievable chunks.

Set smaller goals to measure your progress; you're also more likely to stay motivated in this way. Achieving your micro goals will boost your positive thinking.

It will reduce your stress if you focus on putting in consistent effort and not just the big picture, which can be overwhelming.

So, how do you make your micro goals work for you?

- Set completion dates for long-term goals and work backward for micro goals. You can also write a daily list of micro goals that will help you stay on track.
- Focus on what you can do now to achieve daily goals. You should measure your micro goals regularly and adjust them.

ACTIVITY—HABIT TRACKER

Decide on a goal for the habit you want to develop. It should be specific, measurable, achievable, relevant, and time-bound (SMART).

Write down your goal below, along with two reasons why you want to develop this habit.

_____

_____

_____

_____

Consider which of your existing habits or routines can act as a trigger or "stack" for your new habit. For example, if you want to start making your bed, you could stack it onto your morning routine after getting dressed. Write down your answer below.

_____

_____

Plan when and where you will practice your new habit. Write down a specific time and location.

_____

_____

Start practicing your new habit according to your plan and record each day's practice. Write down the date, time, and any notes about your experience. This will help you track your progress.

_____

_____

_____

_____

Adjust your plan if you have challenges practicing your habit during the week. If you feel you're making progress, set mini milestones for yourself.

Continue practicing your new habit and track your progress every week for at least three months.

KEY TAKEAWAYS

- Making your bed can be your first small win for the day.
- This can boost your confidence and set a positive tone for the rest of your day.
- Making your bed can be the foundation of a structured morning routine, bringing stability and consistency to your life.
- Small wins, like making your bed, can serve as stepping stones for building other positive habits.
- Habit stacking, popularized by James Clear, involves making a new habit part of your routine by associating it with an established one.
- Habit stacking helps create a sequence of actions that your brain follows on autopilot, making it easier to adopt new habits.
- To create lasting habits, one method that works is reshaping your identity by focusing on the type of person you want to become.
- Start with small habit changes that align with your desired identity and eventually lead to

your main goal.

- Identity-based habits require less reliance on motivation and lead to more consistent results.
- Planning and discipline can also help you turn motivation into action.
- A plan helps you bridge the gap between your desires and the actions you take.
- Intrinsic motivation is the internal drive to do something for personal satisfaction rather than external rewards. Volunteering and connecting daily activities to a larger purpose is a good way to boost intrinsic motivation.
- Cultivate a love of learning, stay curious, and embrace challenges. Continuous learning is important for self-discovery and improved intrinsic motivation.
- Setting challenging yet achievable goals can lead to a sense of accomplishment.
- Micro goals involve breaking down big goals into smaller, manageable micro goals.

In Chapter 2, we will give you tips on how to declutter your mind. In our hectic lives, this is a particularly useful skill, as we often have too much to focus on, and we can become overwhelmed.

CHAPTER 2
DECLUTTERING YOUR MIND

> *Declutter your mind, your heart, your home.*
> *Let go of the heaviness that is weighing you*
> *down. Make your life simple but significant.*

MARIA DEFILLO

L ucy was a teenager whose mind was always in chaos. Between her demanding schoolwork, sport, part-time job, and active social life, her thoughts were becoming seriously tangled, and important things in her life were beginning to fall through the cracks. She knew she should prioritize her schoolwork, but she just had so many interests, and there were other things she wanted to do as well.

One sunny afternoon, Lucy's friend Jake sent her an interesting message. He told her about a program the school was launching to help them declutter their minds. It could help them unleash their hidden potential and focus on their studies. He asked if she was interested in attending the program with him.

Lucy was curious immediately, and she wondered if it would be the answer to her busy and distracted mind. She was even struggling to sleep at night, as she simply couldn't shut down her thoughts. This was making it even more difficult for her to focus at school and on studying for her exams. She agreed to go with Jake.

Lucy and Jake's adventure started the following week as they joined a diverse group of students in the school's library. The decluttering program was led by an eccentric but wise teacher named Mr. Smith. He presented a mind map with various challenges, and the students enjoyed his sense of humor.

Gathering in a circle, Mr. Smith greeted the young students and told them that he would teach them how to navigate the labyrinth of their thoughts.

Their first challenge involved a thought experiment. With their eyes closed, they were instructed to take a deep breath and visualize their minds as cluttered rooms. Lucy pictured her mind as her own chaotic bedroom filled with scattered textbooks, crumpled papers, and discarded soccer gear. She felt her heart starting to beat faster at this cluttered picture in her mind, and she started to feel overwhelmed.

Mr. Smith broke the silence in his soothing voice. He told them they would start the decluttering process by tackling one item at a time and deciding if they would keep or discard it. He told them that this was their opportunity to create space for what genuinely mattered to them. He said they should create a box in their mind for the items they didn't need, as they could then plan to donate this to people who need it.

Lucy started the process by addressing a stack of incomplete school assignments that were stashed on her desk. She realized that the constant worry about unfinished work was a heavy load on her shoulders. She often stressed over them but rarely found the determination to complete them. It was almost as if she was carrying a backpack of unfulfilled obligations that was dragging her down. She visualized herself finishing each assignment, and she felt a sense of liberation as she did.

As Lucy proceeded, her mental room gradually cleared and revealed more space than she ever realized she had before, including a reading nook. She felt as if a breath of fresh air had swept through her mind.

As the weeks passed, Lucy and her friends delved deeper into their quest. They acquired mindfulness techniques, discovered the art of setting goals, and learned to manage their digital lives.

One day, while seated in her newly decluttered mental nook, Lucy realized that her mind was sharper, her focus was better, and the once-over-whelming chaos of thoughts had given way to clarity. She felt as if she was leveling up her game in life.

The program helped Lucy and her friends to develop themselves, brimming with potential and boundless opportunities. They were ready to continue their adventure.

MINDFULNESS PRACTICE

Maybe your mind feels cluttered like Lucy's mind and you don't know if you're coming or going. It can be difficult to stay focused if you've got a full routine, but mindfulness can steer you in the right direction.

When you hear the word "mindfulness," you probably think of it as something complicated only yogis or meditation gurus do. However, it can help you a great deal when it comes to navigating the ups and downs of teenage life.

The power of mindfulness can help you lead a more balanced life. We all have times when we stress a lot in our lives. For example, you could still be worrying about a test you failed last week or if your parents will allow you to attend an upcoming social event. Maybe you're experiencing peer pressure and your mind feels too cluttered for you to think clearly about how you can deal with the situation. Especially in this case, mindfulness can be a pause button that helps you stay fully focused on the present.

If the world seems to rush at you when you get up in the morning, you need to start your day with a mindful morning routine, such as making your bed. You need to get control of your thoughts and habits, as everything else will follow from here. Before you dive into the chaos of school work, assignments, text messages, and emails, making your bed with mindfulness can help you set the tone for a serene morning and a calm day. It also gets you going and moving around, which will help your brain wake up and get ready for action.

Try to think of each movement and fold as you make your bed as a mini meditation session. Focus on straightening your sheets, fluffing your pillows, and tucking in the corners.

The magic of mindfulness is that you're fully present in the moment. When you make your bed mindfully, you're not ruminating about yesterday's problems or worrying about the tasks you have to do tomorrow. Your only focus is right here and now and the order you can create in the chaos that surrounds you. It gives you a sense of control, as you can create order out of chaos.

As a teenager, you often have a lot of chaos in your life, from last-minute assignments to social drama. However, making your bed can help you manage your life, and it sets a positive tone for the rest of your day.

Your bed becomes a canvas, and each pillow fluff and sheet fold is like a brushstroke on it. It allows you to become an artist of organization. When you approach it with mindfulness, it's not just a chore; it's a way to express yourself. Your bed becomes your master-piece, and your mind becomes a bit clearer. Just as you declutter your space, you declutter your thoughts, making room for a calmer and more focused mind.

ROUTINES TO DECLUTTER YOUR MIND

Besides making your bed, there are other useful routines you can follow to declutter your mind. Decluttering your mind is an ongoing process, and you should find the routines that work best for you and that you can fit into your busy schedule.

Practice Mindful Breathing

Find a space where you can sit quietly and comfortably. Close your eyes and take a deep breath through your nose. Hold your breath as you count to four.

After this, exhale slowly through your mouth for a count of six. Repeat this process several times, while you focus only on your breathing.

Keep a Journal

Write down your thoughts, feelings, and worries in a journal. This could be done with a pen in a book with a nice cover such as leather, or you could simply keep a record of your thoughts on one of your digital devices. These days, in our digital world, many people prefer typing to writing.

There is an advantage to writing, though, in that you're forced to think for a longer time about what you're writing down. Maybe you study by making notes? Well, this kind of works in the same way.

The benefit of keeping a journal is that it helps you process and release your emotions and organize your thoughts. This will improve your emotional regulation, which will make it easier to keep your mind clear. Emotional regulation means you don't become overwhelmed by your emotions. You're able to deal with difficult situations by not becoming so mad that you scream and shout or so scared and sad that you start crying.

You could also keep a gratitude journal, in which you write down things you're thankful for each day. This will help you keep your mind clear of negative thoughts, and you'll be less likely to ruminate about stressful and negative events.

Take a Mindful Walk

A great way to clear your mind is to regularly walk in nature. Pay attention to all the sounds and sights around you, as well as the sensations you're feeling. Focus on each step you take. If you get distracted by your thoughts, slowly bring them back to your current reality.

Limit Screen Time

Set boundaries on your screen time, including social media, gaming, and TV.

If you're constantly exposed to screens, your mind can be overwhelmed with information and distractions. Try not to use devices for at least an hour before you go to bed at night.

Do a Digital Detox

It's important to take regular breaks from your devices, especially when you're studying. Put your phone in another room and disconnect from screens to allow your mind to relax.

You should also consider taking longer breaks when you can, for example, going camping in nature with your family for a week when you don't use technology at all. Also, try to fill more of your time with sports and hobbies you enjoy doing.

Try Meditation and Guided Relaxation

Use meditation apps such as Headspace and Calm or online resources for guided relaxation and meditation sessions.

These can help you relax, clear your mind, and manage stress.

Prioritize Tasks

Create a to-do list and prioritize tasks so you're able to focus on one task at a time. There's nothing worse than having a confused mind because you're thinking of what you need to do all at once, which mostly means you end up getting nothing done.

If you have priorities, you'll prevent mental clutter from trying to focus on too much at once.

Eat Mindfully

When you're eating, pay close attention to the taste, texture, and smell of your food.

Eating mindfully helps you to be fully focused on your meal, and you can enjoy it without distractions.

Create a Sleep Routine

Make sure you get enough sleep. Too little sleep can lead to a cluttered mind, and it's just bad for your mental and physical well-being. It could affect your memory as well, and you can feel grumpy throughout the day.

Engage in Physical Activity

Do any sport you enjoy. Moving your body releases endorphins and will help you clear your mind.

Talk It Out

Talking with someone about what's on your mind can relieve mental pressure. Share your thoughts and feelings with a trusted friend, family member, or counselor.

Learn to Say No

It's okay to decline tasks or activities if you're already feeling overwhelmed. Don't overcommit yourself to take part in everything at school. You don't have to take part in every sport or extracurricular activity.

You also don't have to say yes to every social activity or every party you get invited to.

Practice Mindful Self-Compassion

Treat yourself with kindness. Don't be too hard on yourself. Accept that you will make mistakes, as you're only human, and that you can learn from them.

You also need to be aware that your life won't always be easy and that challenges will come your way. Learning to deal with them will help you become more resilient, and you'll be better able to deal with challenges that come your way in the future.

Embrace "Me Time"

Set some time aside every day to do something you love, whether it's reading, writing, or playing music. This will help you relax and reset.

Speak to a Counselor

If you find that your cluttered mind is affecting your daily life and well-being, consider speaking to a counselor.

HOW MEDITATION CAN BENEFIT YOU

Meditation is like having a secret weapon for dealing with stress, keeping focused, and boosting your confidence. Meditation isn't some ancient, boring thing; it's a cool, modern tool that can help you focus and get ahead in your life. Let's take a look at how it can help you in the different areas of your life.

Meditation can benefit you in the following ways:

- It can help you reduce stress. As a teenager, you will often have to deal with academic pressures, social challenges, and self-discovery, which could lead to stress.
- Meditation can also help you improve your focus and concentration. You need sustained focus to deal with all the academic demands in your life. Meditation will improve your

concentration levels and help you navigate through your exams and tests.

- Teenagers experience hormonal changes that can result in mood swings. This can add a lot of additional stress to your life. Meditation can help you regulate your emotions and get through the emotional roller coaster of your teenage years.

- Meditation promotes relaxation, which can help you unwind and sleep better. If you struggle with an irregular sleep pattern, it could cause you to experience more stress and your performance at school could be negatively affected.

- Regular meditation can also boost mental resilience. Your teenage years are a time of significant change and can help you cope with challenges, uncertainties, and other setbacks.

- Meditation also encourages more awareness of the mind-body connection. If your mind is clear, you can focus on what you're feeling in different parts of your body. This heightened awareness can help you care for yourself better and make healthier lifestyle choices, which will also increase your overall sense of well-being.

- Meditation fosters empathy and compassion. It can help you navigate social relationships and handle conflicts with a greater sense of understanding.
- Whether in academics or extracurricular activities, you could have to deal with performance-related anxiety. Meditation gives you the tools to manage anxiety, promoting a more relaxed and confident approach.
- Meditation cultivates mindfulness, which can help you stay present and focused in the current moment. This is also a useful and important skill when it comes to dealing with stress.

WHY MINDFULNESS MATTERS DURING THE TEENAGE YEARS

Mindfulness has become a trendy buzzword for many people, but it's so much more.

As we said before, mindfulness is about being present and fully engaged in your present. You can see it as a type of mental gym that helps you focus and deal with the challenges you could face in your life.

School demands, social pressures, and the quest for self-identity can often leave you feeling overwhelmed, almost as if your brain has been scrambled. Mindfulness can help you become calm within the chaotic storms happening around you. It allows you to pause, take a deep breath, and observe your thoughts and emotions without judgment.

Mindfulness gives you the focus and clarity needed to tackle academic challenges. By focusing on the present moment, you enhance your concentration, making it easier to remember difficult information.

Mindfulness could act as your social compass, helping you build deeper connections with others. By being fully present in your interactions, you develop a genuine understanding of others and become empathetic to their needs. Additionally, mindfulness teaches you to manage your reactions, making it less likely that you'll react to challenges emotionally.

Incorporating mindfulness into your daily routine doesn't mean you have to make major changes to your lifestyle. You can do simple things that are easy to incorporate, such as mindful breathing, short meditation sessions, or mindful walking can seamlessly fit into your schedule. If you can make mindfulness a regular part of your routine, it will be even more effective.

POSITIVE ASSOCIATIONS WITH MAKING YOUR BED

A teenager named James lived in a typical suburban town. Like most of us, he had a love-hate relationship with the alarm clock that woke him up every day. Sometimes, he couldn't resist the temptation to hit the snooze button. However, strangely enough, making his bed in the mornings made it easier for him to get going. He had only started doing so recently and was struggling to keep up with this routine, especially early in the mornings when he was still tired. However, he gradually got used to it.

Slowly, James started to overcome the temptation of staying longer in his warm and comfortable bed in the mornings. Making his bed had become the trigger for his start to the day and it told him to get moving. It was almost like a warm-up exercise before he played a basketball game.

While he made his bed, he paid a lot of attention to what he was doing. He changed the pillowcases and folded his sheets carefully, tugging them under the mattress. James's bed was so neat that it was clear he had put a lot of work into it.

His bedroom became his sanctuary from chaos. whereas before he started his transformation, books used to lay scattered on the floor or his bed was a mess of blankets and pillows. However, when he decided to make his bed every day, he started to get control over the morning madness. He felt comforted stepping into his clean and tidy room after school. His mother even commented on the change and that she was impressed by his newfound maturity.

James stopped feeling that his life was pulling him in all directions. He found a sense of control and accomplishment in the small act of making his bed.

On days when it felt as if the weight of his responsibilities felt unbearable, making his bed got his groggy brain going and made him believe that he could handle his day. Making his bed became part of his morning routine, like brushing his teeth.

Like James, it might feel as if your life is hectic and you simply have too much chaos to deal with. Choose to focus on something small or a simple activity to get you going in the right direction.

We challenge you to think of making your bed as a reset button. It's almost like dealing with the chaos in your life and giving yourself a fresh start. It's a new chapter for you and can help you lead a more structured life.

WORKSHEET—DECLUTTER YOUR MIND

This worksheet will guide you through a series of exercises to help you declutter your mind, which help you reduce your stress and can help you focus on your schoolwork and the other important things in your life.

Mindful Breathing (5 minutes)

Close your eyes and take a few deep breaths. Focus on your breathing. Let go of your distracting thoughts as you inhale and exhale. Concentrate only on your breathing. Write down any thoughts or worries that you have during the exercise.

_____

_____

_____

_____

Identify Your Thoughts (10 minutes)

Write down any thoughts, worries, or feelings that are cluttering your mind. Be honest with yourself and try to write down as much as possible.

_____

_____

_____

_____

Journaling Prompts (15 minutes)

Choose one of the prompts below and write about your feelings in your journal.

- Describe a recent challenge and how you handled it.
- Write about something that has been on your mind lately.
- Share a moment that made you smile.
- Think about a situation that made you feel stressed or overwhelmed.
- Write about something you're grateful for.

_____

_____

_____

_____

Self-Compassion Message (5 minutes)

Write an encouraging and kind message to yourself, almost as if you're speaking to one of your friends.

_____

_____

_____

_____

Gratitude Journaling (5 minutes)

List three things you're grateful for in your life. Reflect on the positive moments and aspects of your life that make you happy.

_____

_____

_____

Reflection (5 minutes)

Think about your experience. How did this exercise make you feel? Have your thoughts or emotions changed? Write more about this.

_____

_____

_____

_____

Mindful Goal-Setting (5 minutes)

Set a mindfulness goal for yourself. How can you incorporate mindfulness and decluttering your mind into your daily life?

_____

_____

_____

_____

KEY TAKEAWAYS

- Making the bed becomes a trigger for the start of your day and a warm-up exercise for your mind.
- The act of making your bed will empower you and help you to tackle your hectic life with confidence.
- Your brain will start to associate it with a sense of control and accomplishment.
- Making the bed acts as a reset button, providing a fresh start and structure to your day.

In Chapter 3, we will look at how you can practice self-care by taking care of your physical space.

CHAPTER 3
OWNERSHIP AND SELF-CARE

Self-care is how you take your power back.

LALAH DELIA

Every morning, Sarah would take a few minutes to make her bed. For her, it wasn't about tidying up but, rather, a form of self-care.

Sarah regarded her room as her sanctuary. She decorated it with posters of her favorite bands. She had shelves filled with books and a desk full of art supplies. The centerpiece of her room was her bed. She was especially careful about how she straightened her sheets, fluffed her pillows, and tucked in the corners. For her, this was a self-care ritual.

One afternoon, her friend Alice came to hang out with her. They spent a lot of time chatting, and Alice asked her if it wasn't a hassle to make her bed so meticulously and keep her room so neat.

Sarah smiled and told her that she felt that her room, and especially her bed, was a reflection of how she values herself and her surroundings. She said that when she made her bed and kept her room neat, she was sending a message to herself that she deserved a clean and organized space. This was actually her favorite form of self-care.

Alice struggled to understand this idea, so Sarah explained further. She explained to her friend that she saw her room almost as if it were her personal world and that it held her dreams, emotions, and memories. By making her bed, she was giving herself the message that she and her space mattered in the bigger scheme of things.

Alice thought that Sarah's perspective made sense. It made her realize that self-care could come in many different forms, and she decided to start making her bed every day going forward.

Sarah's story is a reminder to us that we should value our space as we value ourselves and that we can find self-care in our simple daily acts.

Let's look at how taking care of your physical space can be regarded as a form of self-care.

SELF-CARE THROUGH TAKING CARE OF YOUR PHYSICAL SPACE

Taking care of the physical space in which you find yourself daily is a visible and practical form of self-care.

A tidy environment sets the stage for a harmonious and stress-free life, where you can focus on your physical, emotional, and mental well-being. You're investing in your own well-being by investing time and effort into your environment.

First of all, taking care of your physical space has a positive effect on your psychological well-being. It boosts your mental health, reducing your stress and anxiety levels and helping you feel less over-whelmed.

When you walk into your tidy bedroom after a hard day at school, you're just so much more likely to feel relaxed sooner.

Keeping your physical space in order gives you a sense of control over your surroundings. It tells you that you're in charge and capable of managing your life, which boosts your self-esteem and confidence.

Keeping your physical space organized is also a powerful tool for personal development. It tells your subconscious mind that you are capable, in control, and that you deserve a harmonious and efficient environment. This also helps you build your self-esteem and tackle life's challenges with renewed purpose.

When you take the time to tidy up and organize your physical space, you're playing an active role in improving your environment. This sense of agency is empowering. It communicates to your subconscious mind that you can effect positive change in your life. In essence, you're telling yourself that you can make any kind of difference that you want to make.

Completing tasks related to maintaining your space —such as making your bed, decluttering, or organizing your belongings—provides visible evidence that you can accomplish things. You may think these achievements are trivial, but they're actually very important.

Disorder and clutter in your physical space can mirror the chaos or disarray in your life. By tackling these issues, you demonstrate your commitment to changing your life to be more organized. As you see your space become neater and more organized, you gain a greater sense of control over the chaos in other areas of your life.

Decluttering and organizing means you also have to choose what to keep, what to discard, and how to arrange your belongings.

Making these types of decisions is also an opportunity to practice and develop your decision-making skills. As you improve at making these choices, you'll also become more confident in making decisions in other areas of your life.

An organized environment minimizes distractions, making it easier to concentrate on tasks and goals. This improved focus allows you to complete tasks more efficiently, which, in turn, reinforces your sense of competence and capability.

Keeping your physical space in order creates a positive feedback loop. As you notice the benefits it brings to your life, such as reduced stress and increased efficiency, you are motivated to continue maintaining your orderly environment. This ongoing commitment to self-care and organization further enhances your self-esteem and confidence.

The act of maintaining an organized space can also be seen as a form of personal growth. It shows that you're committed to improving yourself and growing as a person.

Overwhelmed Teenager Finds a Sense of Balance Through Decluttering

Lily was a busy high school student with big dreams. Between classes, extracurricular activities, and social commitments, she was always busy, and she eventually started to feel exhausted.

One afternoon, while scrolling through her social media feed, Lily stumbled upon an article about the benefits of decluttering and creating a peaceful sanctuary in her own bedroom. She liked the idea because she needed a space where she could relax, recharge, and find peace.

Lily decided to embark on a mission to transform her chaotic room into a serene sanctuary, but she knew it was going to be a long and difficult job.

She started by clearing her room of clutter, donating old clothes, and organizing her school materials. The more she cleaned, the freer she felt. She felt liberated and like a weight had been lifted off her shoulders.

With her room now in order, Lily turned her attention to her surroundings. She added some colorful pillows and a few potted plants and created a small meditation corner next to her bed. She placed a string of fairy lights on her room's walls, and they cast a warm and inviting glow. She felt the room slowly becoming her retreat from the outside world, and she was comfortable to unwind and relax there.

As time passed, Lily noticed that her new sanctuary helped her relax even on her busiest days. Her room became her safe haven, a place where she could read, meditate, or take a break from the chaos.

Lily's improved surroundings also helped her become more productive. With fewer distractions and a calm atmosphere, she found it easier to focus on her schoolwork. Her grades improved, she gained confidence, and she felt more accomplished.

Lily used to struggle with allergies, and her physical health improved. Her newly decluttered space reduced the risk of allergies, illnesses, and accidents. She also no longer struggled to find what she needed in her room.

She realized that the transformation of her room had been a transformation of herself. She had learned the value of self-care in the everyday act of creating a clean and serene space.

The once overwhelmed and exhausted teenager had become a balanced and tranquil person. Lily's sanctuary had become a place of refuge and rejuvenation, reminding her that she could find peace and self-care even in the busiest times of her life.

ACCOMPLISHMENT CASCADE WORKSHEET

This worksheet will help you set the stage for a productive and awesome day.

- Choose one small task you can do right away in the morning. It could be making your bed, taking a shower, or having a healthy breakfast.
- Complete the task. As you do it, pay attention to how it makes you feel. Do you feel a sense of accomplishment?
- Write down how you felt after completing the task. Did it make you feel good?

_____

Now, think about what you'd like to do next. What are the next small steps you can take?

Complete the next task. The feeling of accomplishment from the first task will motivate you to keep going.

Keep tackling one small task after another. The accomplishment will build up like a cascade of positivity.

KEY TAKEAWAYS

- Making your bed can be a form of self-care, indicating that you value yourself.
- An organized space communicates to your subconscious mind that you are capable, in control, and deserving of a harmonious environment.
- Decluttering and organizing involve making choices, and you get to practice your decision-making skills.

- An organized environment minimizes distractions, and you'll be better able to focus on your tasks and goals.

In Chapter 4, we will consider how a healthy environment can be a form of self-care.

CHAPTER 4
HEALTHY ENVIRONMENT

Breathe. Let go. And remind yourself that this very moment is the only one you know you have for sure.

OPRAH WINFREY

One day, as Maya browsed through social media, she stumbled upon an article that caught her attention.

The article spoke about the benefits of maintaining a tidy and healthy living space. Maya had always considered her room a reflection of her inner self, and she was excited by the idea of creating a sanctuary in her bedroom. Her room had lately become very messy, as she was always busy with her studies, and she didn't get much time for cleaning. There were also way too many unnecessary items in the room, and Maya had allergies that she wanted to get under control.

She started improving her room by making her bed every morning. It gave her an immediate sense of control, and she felt less stressed and anxious. Her room wasn't chaotic anymore, and she could relax there away from the outside world.

Maya's efforts to improve her bedroom didn't stop at making her bed. She decided to declutter her space, and she donated her old clothes and organized her school materials. The more she cleaned, the lighter she felt, as if a weight had been lifted from her shoulders. Her room became an inviting, beautiful place, and her allergies also improved.

Her improved surroundings helped her focus on her schoolwork, leading to better grades and increased confidence. She had discovered the power of managing her living space as getting control of her life and not letting stress control her.

Her newly decluttered space improved allergies, illnesses, and accidents. She no longer wasted time searching for lost items in the chaos of her room. The transformation of her living space had transformed her own life.

Like Maya, you can find self-care in your daily tasks, which will help you maintain your physical, emotional, and mental health. Let's take a closer look at how you can do this.

SELF-CARE AS PART OF YOUR DAILY TASKS

Self-care is an important part of your morning routine. Start your day off with a mindful morning routine. Instead of rushing around, enjoy your breakfast and warm shower slowly, taking some moments to breathe deeply. This will help you get into a positive mindset for the day.

When you sit down to eat breakfast, don't just swallow down your cereal or toast hastily. Take a moment to enjoy each bite. Feel the texture, taste the flavors, and appreciate the food that's giving you the energy to conquer the day. You'll be surprised at how this can make your breakfast way more enjoyable.

Instead of rushing through your shower, focus on every moment. Feel the warm water on your skin and let it relax you. Take some deep breaths and let the steamy shower wake you up. You'll be refreshed and ready to get going.

Before you run out the door and rush to school, pause for a minute and take some deep breaths. Inhale slowly, feel the air filling your lungs and then exhale. It's like a mini mind reset. This will help you feel more focused and less stressed.

Food, hydration, and exercise are essential parts of self-care.

Healthy Eating

Eating right is not about diets or being super strict; it's about treating your body well and enjoying good food. Starting your day with a healthy, delicious breakfast as part of your self-care routine will set the tone for the rest of the day.

Your brain needs food rich in nutrients, like fruits, veggies, and whole grains, to help it work smarter.

Ever had a sugar rush followed by a crash? It's an awful feeling, and it could put an end to your productivity for a few hours if your mind gets foggy. That's why eating nutritious meals is essential. It keeps your energy steady throughout the day, so you don't have those ups and downs.

Healthy eating can also do wonders for your skin. You can use all the skin creams you want, but if you don't eat healthy food and give your body what it needs, you simply won't have healthy skin.

What you eat can affect your mood. Skip the junk food and go for meals that give you energy and help your moods stay stable.

Regular Exercise

Exercise will help you build muscle and feel great. When you exercise, your body releases endorphins, which lift your mood and make you feel awesome after working out.

Exercise is your secret weapon against school stress and teenage drama. Whether it's going for a jog, dancing, or playing a sport, it helps you blow off steam.

You might think exercising makes you tired, but it actually does the opposite. Regular physical activity gives you more energy and will help you get through your days. Exercise can also help you think more clearly, and will help you ace that presentation or exam.

Hydration

It's super important to drink enough water during the day, even though it's easy to forget to do this. If you get dehydrated, you'll feel tired and sluggish.

When you're hydrated, you're more alert and ready to tackle your day.

Staying hydrated will help your skin look fresh and hydrated. It's like a natural beauty secret.

When it's hot outside or you're being active, your body needs extra hydration. Drinking water helps you cool down and prevents overheating.

Drinking enough water also helps you concentrate better. You'll ace that math problem or get good marks for your essays.

Time Management, Breaks, and Relaxation

As a teenager, it can become overwhelming to juggle all the different aspects of your life. Effective time management can make your life easier in many ways.

When you plan your time well, you're less likely to feel rushed or panicked about looming deadlines. It's not ideal to pull all-nighters before exams and before projects are due, as you'll be too tired to focus properly, and you won't be able to deliver quality work.

Good time management also means you'll have more time for the fun things in your life. When you organize your tasks efficiently, you'll find you have more time for hobbies, gaming, or hanging out with your friends.

Managing your time wisely means you can focus on studying and understanding your subjects better. You can get better grades without cramming for your exams.

Breaks and Relaxation

Your teenage years can be quite intense, with a lot happening all at once. That's why taking breaks and finding moments to relax can help you recharge. Short breaks are like pressing the reset button for your brain. They help you refocus and re-energize. Even a quick five-minute break can make a huge difference.

Your mental health is just as important as your physical health. Taking time to relax, whether through meditation or just enjoying a peaceful walk, can reduce anxiety and improve your overall mood.

You might feel like you need to go full speed all the time, but that can lead to burnout. Regular breaks ensure you don't hit that wall, allowing you to keep going at a steady pace. Remember, if you burn out, you'll experience even more stress if you're unable to do anything for a while, and you'll have a lot of work to catch up on.

When you're relaxed, you're also more creative. When your mind isn't on overdrive, you're more likely to come up with good ideas for your creative projects.

So, as a teenager, time management helps you stay on top of your busy schedule, and taking breaks keeps you in good mental and emotional shape. This is all part of your self-care routine and will help you enjoy life to the fullest.

Positive Affirmations and Self-Compassion

You may sometimes not be that confident and even fall prey to negative thinking. Using positive affirmations can help you put your inner voice on the right track.

These affirmations are like little pep talks you give yourself. For example, if you believe you're going to fail at something and that you can't do it, you need to turn these thoughts around and tell yourself that you will be successful. When you're constantly telling yourself you're strong, smart, and capable, you will start believing it. You'll be able to achieve amazing things when you believe it.

Affirmations can give you the confidence and courage to tackle anything new in your life successfully. A great trick is to write down some of them as part of your daily self-care routine and to put them up where you can see them, for example, on the walls or the fridge. They'll remind you to stay positive, even when things are going rough in your life. You'll find it easier to maintain an optimistic outlook during tough times.

You could also feel like you're sometimes experiencing a roller coaster of emotions. It's during times like these that you need to have compassion for yourself. Treat yourself in the same way you would treat your best friend when they're going through a bad time.

You need to accept that it's okay to make mistakes and that you're learning and growing as a person. Everyone makes mistakes, and you should see them as growth opportunities.

Celebrate all the successes in your life, even if you think they're small and not all that important. Be proud of yourself when you achieve things, such as doing well on a test.

Remember that the teenage years are an emotional time in most people's lives. If you're kind to yourself, it's much easier to get through them in one piece. Don't beat yourself up if you feel sad, angry, or frustrated at times. Everyone is going through these emotions—just be gentle with yourself during these times. This will also help you become more resilient and bounce back from setbacks faster.

SELF-CARE ROUTINE WORKSHEET

This worksheet can help you create a personalized self-care plan.

Self-Reflection

Before you begin the process, you need to think about what makes you feel happy and relaxed.

What are the activities or hobbies that make you feel happy and relaxed?

_____

_____

What are the things or situations that stress you out or make you feel overwhelmed?

_____

_____

What type of exercise do you enjoy doing or have always wanted to try?

_____

_____

What are your favorite ways to relax and unwind?

_____

_____

Identify Self-Care Activities

Inspired by the self-reflection you've done, write down some self-care activities you're interested in doing. These can be daily, weekly, or monthly practices.

Physical Self-Care

_____

Example: Yoga, walking, or dancing

Emotional Self-Care

_____

Examples: Breathing exercises, writing in your journal, talking to a friend

Mental Self-Care

_____

Example: Reading, brain games, or learning something new

Social Self-Care

_____

Example: Spending time with family and friends or virtually meeting with friends

Spiritual Self-Care

_____

Examples: Attending a place of worship or meditating

Create Your Self-Care Schedule

When you plan your self-care routine, you should consider your daily and weekly schedule. Be realistic about how much time you have available for self-care. You should be flexible and adjust your time, for example, if you need more time for your studies. During school holidays, you'll have more time to practice your self-care.

_____

_____

Daily Self-Care: Identify one or more self-care activities you can do daily. These should be relatively quick and easy to incorporate into your routine.

Example: Take a 15-minute walk after studying.

_____

_____

Weekly Self-Care: Choose activities you can do once a week, perhaps on the weekends or when you have more free time.

Example: Finish a painting you've been working on or go on a hike with friends.

_____

_____

Monthly Self-Care: For activities that take more time, plan them once a month or as occasional treats.

Example: Go on a weekend camping trip.

_____

_____

Set Self-Care Goals

Set goals for your self-care. What do you want to achieve through this routine?

_____

_____

Short-Term Goals: What would you like to accomplish in the next month?

Example: I want to become more confident and less anxious.

_____

_____

Long-Term Goals: What do you hope to achieve over the next few months or years?

Example: I want to grow as a person, be successful at my studies, and get a good job.

_____

_____

Implement and Review

Start incorporating your self-care routine into your life. Track your progress in your journal and change your routine if you feel there are ways to make it more effective and enjoyable.

KEY TAKEAWAYS

- Self-care is essential for staying healthy and should be part of your daily routine.

- A mindful morning routine can set a positive tone for your day. For example, you should take time to enjoy your breakfast.
- Eat nutritious meals to sustain energy and support your physical and emotional health.
- Exercise, such as jogging, dancing, or playing a sport, can boost your mood and provide physical and mental benefits.
- Hydration is crucial for staying alert, looking after your skin, and helping you concentrate on schoolwork or other tasks you have to do.
- Effective time management can help you reduce your stress levels and give you more time for relaxation and leisure activities.
- Taking short breaks throughout the day can help you recharge and refocus.
- Positive affirmations are like pep talks that boost your self-confidence and help you maintain a positive outlook.
- Practicing self-compassion involves being kind to yourself, acknowledging your accomplishments, and embracing personal growth.

In Chapter 5, we're going to look at how you can create visual order in your bedroom by creating different zones.

CHAPTER 5
VISUAL ORDER AND YOUR ROOM

> *Making your bed is a small act of discipline that can have a big impact on your life.*

JORDAN PETERSON

n this chapter, we'll look at how visual order can impact your daily life. Imagine this: You and your best friends decide to have a movie night. You invite them over, and as you open the door to your room, they're met with a chaotic scene. Your clothes are scattered everywhere on the bed and floor, and your sheets are a mess. How does that make you feel? Now, picture the opposite: a tidy space, a made bed, and an atmosphere of calm. That's the magic of visual order, and in this chapter, we'll explore how it goes beyond clean aesthetics, enhancing your relationships.

YOUR SAFE HAVEN

Your room isn't just four walls and a bed; it's a hub of shared experiences, laughter, and late-night talks if you're lucky enough to share it with siblings, room-mates, or friends.

Imagine your room as a blank canvas waiting to be painted with beautiful, shared memories. Whether it's a sleepover with friends, a study session, or just hanging out after school, your room will be your safe haven. Visual order ensures that all your friends will feel welcome and valued in this shared space. After all, you want everyone to enjoy their time with you.

A made bed and an organized space send a message not only to others but also to yourself.

It's not just about creating nice photos for Instagram; it's a message that you respect others and care about the relationship you share with them. When you invite people into a tidy space, it shows that you care about them and respect them. You want them to spend a great time with you in a space that feels good.

Think about a time you hung out in someone's room. How did it make you feel? Was it cozy and inviting? You probably didn't have to find your way around piles of clothes.

Visual order makes it easier to connect, as it makes everything more enjoyable.

PRACTICAL TIPS TO CREATE ORDER IN YOUR BEDROOM

Keeping a visually organized bedroom can contribute to a more peaceful and productive living space. Here are some practical tips that you can use to create order in your bedroom.

Declutter Regularly

Decluttering regularly is one of the most important things you can do when it comes to creating visual order. It isn't just about having a clean room; it's about creating a space that reflects who you are right now.

So, how should you go about this? Book out some time in your digital calendar, or any other type of calendar you decide to use, to declutter. Get rid of items that you no longer need or want. If you have clothes or other items that are still in good condition but you can't use them any longer, you can donate or sell them. Remember, the shirt or dress that you don't wear anymore could potentially become someone else's favorite item.

You should notice how the decluttering process makes you feel. Do you feel lighter, as if you've dropped unnecessary baggage? Hopefully, you now have plenty of space to move around without tripping over things.

As a teenager, you're constantly growing and changing. Your style and interests will change a lot during these years of your life. Decluttering is important, as it helps your room match the current version of yourself. Now, you can make new memories in your room.

Decluttering isn't always that exciting, but you can make it more so by rewarding yourself after every session. Treat yourself with something—be it more gaming time or a snack. You're acknowledging to yourself that you've done the job well.

If you've got friends with the same struggle with clutter, you can make it a group effort. You can swap items, give each other decorating tips, or just have a decluttering party together. You could turn a task that you may usually find boring into a fun social event.

Organize Storage Spaces

This is super exciting, as you'll have so much more space that you can use once you're done. Invest in storage solutions like bins, baskets, and shelves to keep your belongings neatly organized. Drawer dividers can help you separate your clothes and other accessories.

This probably sounds strange, but you need an effective inventory management system. Bins and baskets can help you keep your clothes and other important stuff sorted. Think how nice it will be not having to search everywhere for an item of clothing when you want to wear it.

You will get better at organizing your space the more you practice it. It's the same manner as with any other skill.

Have you ever tried to find a small item that got lost in your messy room? With organized storage, you'll never end up frantically searching for something before you have to leave the house.

If you share a room, organizing is like teaming up in multiplayer mode. Coordinate with your siblings or roommates to create a space that works for everyone.

Zone Your Room

Creating different zones in your bedroom means you can even create your own special hangout spot. Think about it almost as creating different levels in your favorite game.

Designate a Study Area

Create a zone with a desk and good lighting for your studies. Personalize it with cool stationery, maybe a motivational poster—it needs to be a place where you can focus and your productivity will ultimately thrive.

Create a Relaxation Corner

You can create a comfortable corner with a chair or cushions as your relaxation zone. Here, you can unwind after a long day, read a book, or just relax. Add some soft lighting and some decorations to make it your favorite chill-out spot.

Use Vertical Space

Instill wall-mounted shelves or hooks to maximize vertical storage. You could also consider a tall bookshelf or a wardrobe to make use of vertical space efficiently.

Consider Your Sleeping Space

Your bed is the main place where you will recharge. You need it comfortable and inviting. Make your bed every morning to start the day fresh. This is where you'll get the energy to deal with the challenges the day is going to throw at you.

Establish a Routine for Cleaning

While making your bed has now become part of your good habits and morning routine, it's also good to have a more long-term cleaning routine that will help you keep your room in good condition. It doesn't have to happen every day, but you could at least have a weekly cleaning routine.

Do Some Digital Organization

Organizing your digital devices, charging cables, and other items should be part of your decluttering exercise. Another part of this is that you should declutter your digital files to keep your virtual space tidy.

When it comes to cable organizers, you have quite a selection to choose from. There are velcro straps, all kinds of cool clips, and even a cable organizer box.

Cable organizers can help you untangle your charging cables. Make sure all your cables are neatly secured so you don't have to struggle and fight with cables when you need to charge your devices.

You can also become more organized by adding labels to your items. A small tag or label on each cable makes it clear which one powers up your gaming gear, phone, or whatever other devices you might use. You won't have to guess any longer.

Create a charging station for all your gadgets. This will be a safe haven for your devices to rest and recharge. Make sure you have a designated spot for everything—you don't want to hunt for your tablet or headphones. Also, arrange your charging station where you can easily reach it.

Every now and then, do a tech check. Make sure all your cables are in order and nothing's frayed or worn out. This would be a type of routine maintenance to make sure everything runs smoothly.

You can even color code your cables if you think this will work for you. Assign different colors to different devices or functions. It makes it so much easier to identify items, and it just looks cool.

Use Dual-Purpose Furniture

Furniture with different functions can also save you space in your bedroom. For example, a bed with large storage drawers underneath it can also be used for storing items.

Label Everything

Label storage containers, drawers, and shelves to easily identify the contents. This can help keep your school supplies, accessories, and personal items organized.

Limit Your Decor

Don't overcrowd your room with all kinds of decorations. Choose a few items that are meaningful to you.

Keep surfaces clear, especially where you need to study and work. Clutter also tends to attract a lot of dust.

Assess Clothing

Regularly assess your wardrobe to see if there are clothes you haven't worn in a long time that you can donate to others who might still be able to use them. Rotate seasonal clothing and donate items that are no longer worn or don't fit.

Recycle

Setting up a recycling system in your space won't only help you keep your room clean, but it's also a great way to contribute to saving the planet.

First of all, you need at least three bins: one for recycling, one for items to be donated, and one for trash.

You'll find that the trash bin is only for items that can't be recycled or donated, and it should contain the fewest items if you're going about your recycling in the right way. This could be broken items and food wrappers.

These bins should also be labeled, and it's important that you check them regularly. The various items should be in the correct bins.

You could always share your recycling mission with your friends. Encourage them to also start recycling systems and you can work toward saving the planet together. You can lead by example to them and be a sustainability role model.

VISUAL ORDER ACTIVITIES

Set a date for your monthly decluttering sessions and fill out the dates on the calendar below.

Decluttering Calendar

- **January**
- **February**
- **March**
- **April**
- **May**
- **June**
- **July**
- **August**
- **September**
- **October**
- **November**
- **December**

Identify three areas in your room that need decluttering and write them down below.

_____

_____

Make a list of things you no longer need and write them down below.

_____

_____

Make a list of items that are still in good condition that you can donate or sell.

_____

_____

Make a list of storage solutions you need. This could be shelves, bins, and baskets.

_____

_____

Create a designated zone plan for your bedroom. Plan specific areas for different activities.

Study Area

_____

Relaxation Corner

_____

Sleeping Space

_____

How will you personalize your zones to reflect your style? Write about it below.

_____

_____

Write out label bins below to make your organizing easier.

_____

_____

Write down when you will do your regular checks on your digital items.

_____

_____

KEY TAKEAWAYS

- Visual order can impact your daily life and relationships.
- A messy room can create chaos, while an organized space will give you a more positive experience.
- Your room can be an enjoyable place of shared experiences, laughter, and talks.
- Visual order ensures a welcoming atmosphere for friends, fostering positive relationships.
- A tidy space sends a message of respect and care to others and yourself.
- Create study and relaxation zones to personalize your space. It's easier to manage regular decluttering if you have designated areas in your room.

- Utilize vertical space with wall-mounted shelves and hooks. Even a small room can look tidy if space is used well.
- Keep to a routine of making your bed every morning.
- Furniture with multiple functions can also save you space.
- Set up a recycling system with separate bins for recycling, donations, and trash.
- Encourage your friends to adopt a recycling mindset.

In Chapter 6, we're going to look at the various things that can give you psychological comfort.

CHAPTER 6
PSYCHOLOGICAL COMFORT

A serene mind finds solace in a tidy space.

UNKNOWN

Lisa was a girl who managed to achieve psychological comfort by cultivating good habits, even though she had a rather chaotic high school life.

Lisa usually started her day with a morning routine that included making her bed and mindful breathing exercises. This also helped her set positive goals for the rest of her day.

This simple act grounded her in the present moment, providing a foundation for psychological well-being. As she navigated through the challenges of school,

Lisa discovered the power of maintaining order and tidiness in her personal space. Her neatly organized study desk and bedroom became her sanctuaries, offering a refuge from the chaos of her day.

Beyond physical order, Lisa also understood the importance of mental clarity. She obtained this by writing in her journal. This practice allowed her to declutter her mind, and she also developed a deeper understanding of herself.

Lisa also surrounded herself with positive influences and made friends who uplifted and supported her. She shared fun times with her friends, but they also supported each other through the challenges of adolescence.

In Lisa's life, the threads of good habits, order, and tidiness wove together to create a canvas of psychological comfort. Her routine, tidy environment, and strong support network helped her to build strength and resilience.

Lisa also discovered that psychological comfort was an ongoing journey—one where the harmony she sought was the result of the symphony of her daily choices and experiences.

So, what is the psychological comfort that Lisa experienced? We can describe it as a state of well-being and ease within your own mind. You achieve this state when you feel secure and content and you achieve a sense of inner peace. It's also a combination of emotional, mental, and environmental factors. Positive thoughts, healthy habits, a sense of control, and a supportive environment contribute to this state of comfort. You achieve this dynamic sense of balance when you feel emotionally secure and also equipped to handle life's challenges with resilience.

GOOD HABITS AND PSYCHOLOGICAL COMFORT

There are several ways in which good habits can create psychological comfort. A steady daily routine with times and places for everything you need to do throughout your day creates a comforting predictability and reduces the stress of the unknown. This will give you a greater sense of control over your life.

Dealing with the stress of the unknown every day can spoil your day before it has even started. When you have a clear plan, you know what to expect— from your morning routine to your study sessions and relaxation time before bed. Your mind will be so much clearer when you don't have to deal with uncertainties and surprises.

Having a routine is stabilizing and can help you give structure to your life. Imagine that you have dedicated study hours where you give all your attention to your studies and your projects. This not only improves your academic performance but also helps you gain more control over your educational journey.

Having control over aspects of your day can help you feel more empowered. It's like being the captain of your ship, making decisions that influence your academic and personal development.

Picture having dedicated study hours where you focus on your assignments and projects. This not only improves your academic performance but also gives you a sense of control over your learning. You're actively shaping your educational journey.

Planning your time can also give you a great sense of psychological comfort. If you have planned properly, you'll have fewer surprises to deal with and your life will be less stressful.

Your planner or digital tools can help you organize your tasks and set goals to manage your time; It's up to you to empower yourself to work toward your dreams in a way that fits your unique journey.

As a teenager, you could often feel as if you have too many things to juggle at once. There is your schoolwork, extracurriculars, busy social life, and personal interests. It's easy to feel overwhelmed, but proper planning, with the aid of digital tools, can help you get back on track.

When you break down your big dreams into small, achievable goals, it's like turning a massive puzzle into bite-sized pieces. Each small win adds up, creating a sense of accomplishment. This isn't just about being organized; it's about building your own road map through the chaos of adolescence.

Your road map will give you a greater sense of psychological comfort. It reduces stress, brings order to the chaos, and lets you focus on what truly matters to you. So, whether it's acing that math test, nailing your soccer game, or working on your art project, your road map keeps you on track and will help you become more confident.

Improved Sleep Quality

One of the most important things you will need as a teenager, and what will contribute to your psychological comfort, is quality sleep.

You should have a bedtime routine that allows you to go to bed at the same time every day. This will help your body and brain relax. If your sleep patterns are too irregular, it could influence your mood and concentration. Healthy sleep habits will help you improve your mental and emotional resilience.

So, how does quality sleep play a role in your psychological comfort? It can do so in the following ways:

- Getting good sleep reduces your stress levels. Adequate sleep helps regulate stress hormones, and you'll feel calmer. When you're well-rested, you're better equipped to cope with daily stressors, and you'll also feel less anxious.
- Quality sleep also helps you to be emotionally more resilient, as you're better able to manage and regulate your emotions. You'll be more stable emotionally and less prone to mood swings.
- Getting enough sleep will improve your cognitive functioning. Sleep is important for your memory, as well as problem-solving and decision-making skills. A well-rested mind is sharper, more focused, and better equipped to handle difficult mental tasks. Your overall psychological well-being will be better.
- If you don't sleep enough, you'll be more likely to develop mood disorders, including

depression and anxiety. Quality sleep contributes to the production of neurotransmitters that promote a positive mood and will help you feel more optimistic and content.

- Sleep is important for sustaining your attention and concentration. When you've had a good night's sleep, you're more likely to stay focused on tasks, and you'll also have to strain less when it comes to completing them.

- Your brain processes and consolidates your emotions from the day while you're asleep. This will help you stay healthier emotionally, as you'll be able to approach challenges with a clearer perspective.

Resilience Can Increase Your Psychological Comfort

Learning resilience can significantly increase your sense of psychological comfort by equipping you with the tools and mindset to deal with the challenges you might have to face in your life. Resilience is your ability to bounce back from setbacks, cope with stress, and adapt to difficult situations.

Learning resilience can contribute to psychological comfort in the following ways:

- Resilience involves developing the skills to regulate and deal with your emotions during difficult times. By understanding and controlling your emotional responses, you can foster a greater sense of calm and stability, contributing to psychological comfort.

- Resilient people are adaptable and open to change. If you can learn to embrace and navigate change, it will help you feel less anxious when you have to deal with uncertainty, and you'll be in a more comfortable psychological space overall.

- Resilience is also linked to having a positive outlook in life. By focusing on your strengths, opportunities, and solutions rather than the challenges you have to deal with, you'll develop a more positive outlook. This optimism contributes to a sense of comfort and confidence in your ability to handle difficulties.

- A diverse set of coping strategies also usually leads to improved resilience. These can be cognitive or behavioral strategies that help you to deal with stress better.

- When you're resilient, you believe in your ability to overcome challenges. You feel confident and empowered, which contributes to psychological comfort because you believe you can deal with whatever comes your way.

- Resilient people often have strong social connections. Knowing that you have a support system in times of need creates a sense of security and comfort. Sharing your experiences and asking others for their advice could also give you a higher sense of psychological comfort.

- Resilience involves developing effective problem-solving skills. If you're able to approach challenges with a solution-oriented mindset, you'll feel less helpless and more in control of your situation, which promotes psychological comfort.

- Resilience often incorporates practices like mindfulness, which involves being present in the moment without judgment. This will reduce your stress and anxiety, which will lead to a more comfortable psychological state.

- Resilience is closely tied to personal growth and learning from experiences. Embracing challenges as opportunities for growth will give you a sense of purpose and will help you to reframe challenges in a more positive light.

- Resilience also allows you to see setbacks as part of the learning process rather than as failures. This will reduce your fear of failure, and you'll be in a more comfortable space psychologically.

Positive Relationships

Positive relationships play an important part in your life. They can influence your sense of well-being and psychological comfort. Healthy relationships with your friends and family will contribute to your well-being.

Louise was a young teenage girl who was fortunate to be part of a warm and supportive family. Family dinners were a cherished tradition, where they shared the day's adventures and laughed together. Louise's parents, Emily and Mark, created an environment of open communication and trust. This made Louise feel a deep sense of belonging, as she knew that she was assured of the love and support of her family.

Friendship also played an important role in Louise's future. She had a diverse group of friends, each with unique quirks and qualities. They were all a bit different and highly intelligent, but they formed a tight-knit circle and always supported each other.

They shared dreams, supported each other through challenges, and celebrated victories together. Whether it was doing well in difficult exams or simply making it through a tough day, the camaraderie provided her with psychological comfort.

Louise was also involved in various clubs and activities. The drama club became like a second home to her, which offered her the opportunity for creative expression and also an opportunity to connect with like-minded peers. It gave her a sense of purpose to be part of a larger community. She found a sense of purpose and belonging.

Healthy relationships can help you develop emotional intelligence. If you're able to express and understand your emotions—both your own and those of others—it will help you communicate more effectively, and you'll also be better at resolving conflict.

WORKSHEET: CULTIVATING GOOD HABITS

Section 1: Daily Habits

Morning Routine

List three positive habits you want to include in your morning routine.

_____

_____

Digital Detox

Plan a daily time for your digital detox. Think of activities that can replace your time in front of screens.

Time for Detox

_____

Offline Activities

_____

Healthy Snacking

List three healthy snacks that can become part of your daily routine.

_____

_____

Section 2: Psychological Comfort

Mindfulness Practices

Choose one mindfulness activity to incorporate into your daily routine.

_____

How does this activity make you feel?

_____

Positive Affirmations

Create three positive affirmations you can believe in. You can also write them down on pieces of cardboard and put them up somewhere you can see them every day. Repeat them daily and take note if your mindset changes.

Emotional Check-In

Set a time to do an emotional check-in with yourself every day.

_____

Gratitude Journal

Write down three things for which you're grateful in your gratitude journal.

_____

_____

_____

Section 3: Goal-Setting

Short-Term Goals

Identify three short-term goals you want to achieve in the next month.

_____

_____

Break down each goal into smaller, manageable steps.

_____

_____

Long-Term Aspirations

Envision three long-term goals for yourself. What can you do to get closer to these goals?

Section 4: Social Connection

Quality Time

Plan an activity to connect with friends or family this week.

_____

_____

Is the social connection good for your mental and physical well-being?

_____

_____

Communication Skills

Which aspects of your communication skills do you want to improve? Explain in detail.

_____

_____

How are you going to work at improving your communication skills in your daily interactions?

_____

_____

KEY TAKEAWAYS

- A mindful morning routine can help you set positive goals for the day.
- If your bedroom is neatly organized, it can become your sanctuary and offer you a refuge from the chaos of your daily life.

- Journaling is a great way to declutter your mind, which can also give you mental clarity, self-understanding, and emotional well-being.
- You need to surround yourself with positive influences and build a strong support network of friends who will uplift and support you.
- Fun times and shared challenges contribute to psychological comfort during your challenging teenage years.
- Good habits, order, and tidiness can contribute to a sense of psychological comfort in your life.
- Your routine, tidy environment, and supportive network contribute to your strength and resilience.
- Good habits, such as a steady daily routine, create predictability and reduce stress.
- Breaking down big dreams into small, achievable goals builds a road map that will heighten your sense of psychological comfort.
- Regular sleep patterns reduce stress, enhance emotional resilience, and improve cognitive functioning. It also contributes to psychological comfort.

- Learning resilience will help you bounce back from setbacks and adapt to challenges.
- Resilience fosters emotional regulation, adaptability, a positive outlook, and effective problem-solving skills.
- Healthy relationships with your family and friends will contribute to your well-being and psychological comfort.
- Positive relationships foster emotional intelligence, effective communication, and a sense of belonging.
- Involvement in clubs and activities, such as drama clubs, gives a sense of purpose and belonging.
- A supportive community contributes to psychological comfort and personal development.

In Chapter 7, we're going to look at how personal pride and resilience can help you get ahead and better deal with life.

CHAPTER 7
PERSONAL PRIDE

You are more powerful than you know; you are beautiful just as you are.

MELISSA ETHERIDGE

Self-discovery and daily challenges are important parts of a teenager's daily life. The ordinary act of making your bed can boost your personal pride and self-esteem and also give you more self-respect. In simple words: A neatly made bed will make you feel good about yourself.

Emma was a 16-year-old with big dreams. Her room reflected her creative and fun personality and was both her sanctuary and a place where she could fully express herself. One morning, she was faced with a dilemma: Her room was chaotic after the typical morning rush. Her bed was unmade, and clothes were scattered everywhere.

She was torn between rushing out to school or putting her bedroom together first. Then, she remembered her mother had told her that cleaning her bedroom was a sign of self-respect. If she kept her bedroom in good order, she was telling the universe she deserved to stay in a room that reflected her inner values.

She thought about this as she started working to put her room in order. She quickly transformed her unmade bed into a place of comfort. She fluffed the pillows and smoothed the sheets until she felt as if she had accomplished something. She instantly felt better about herself and what she had to face during the rest of her day.

While doing this ritual every day, Emma felt she had accomplished something. It became clear to her that she could create order from chaos.

Her self-esteem and personal pride improved. Making her bed and cleaning up her personal space has paved the way for her to develop more positive personal habits.

THE POWER OF PERSONAL PRIDE

Personal pride is the secret weapon that will help you manage the ups and downs of teenage life.

Teenage life is unpredictable, and it can almost be like surfing unpredictable waves. You will experience highs, lows, and the occasional disaster. Personal pride helps you to ride out these problems and deal with them. No matter how big the problem, you're capable of dealing with it and staying on your feet. When you're proud of your journey, every challenge becomes an opportunity for fantastic new experiences.

Pride can build your confidence and shield you from the critics in your life. Societal expectations can often be overwhelming when you're a teenager, and personal pride can help you navigate through this. It's like a shield that deflects the negativity you might face from other people and will help you deal with judgment.

How Personal Pride Can Help You Deal With Bullies

Have you had to deal with certain people at school calling you nasty names and trying to make you feel bad about yourself?

Bullies are pretty common, and they thrive on making people feel bad about themselves. However, if you have enough personal pride, this can help you deflect all these negative comments. If you're proud of who you are, their terrible words will bounce off your shield of confidence.

Bullies love to compare, criticize, and make you feel less than. They enjoy seeing your confidence drop, as you'll be less likely to take on their evil behavior. However, if you know that you're not here to fit into other people's mold, you can stand up against them. Their comparisons of you with others won't be as effective if you're proud of your uniqueness. This is showing them that you're not playing the game and you're running your own show.

If you don't have enough personal pride or confidence, you could even end up "bullying" yourself. This may sound strange, but it's pretty easy to do this during the time of social media, which is also popular among teenagers. People usually only put the best aspects of their lives on social media—like when they do well on a test, get a new boyfriend, or make a lot of money. You may start to compare yourself to your friends if you think they're doing so much better than you, and this could send your self-confidence plummeting.

When insults are thrown at you, you should see it as an opportunity to boost your personal pride. Instead of letting words break you down, use them as building blocks to improve your resilience. Level up your game in life and rise above negativity.

Bullies want to take your agency away from you and write your story for you. Personal pride gives the pen back to you. It gives you the confidence to write your own story and to tell the world who you are. Bullies lose their grip on your life when you're proud of your story. You can become the hero of your own life and be the one who is in control.

Another way in which bullies thrive is when you stay silent about what they do to you. Have the confidence to share your experiences—even with adults if you need someone to help you with the situation. When you open up to others, they can help you form a united front against bullying.

This is your support system, and personal pride empowers you to seek their advice. It's not about weakness; it's about tapping into the collective wisdom of your support team, as you can learn from their collective experience how to deal with bullying.

Your friends become your allies in the battle against bullies. Personal pride is the realization that you're not alone in this fight. Bullies often target individuals, thinking it's easier to break them down. If you stand together with others against the bullies, you're less likely to be bullied.

Personal pride is contagious. When you take pride in standing up against bullying, you inspire others to do the same, and, hopefully, you can even create bully-free zones.

Unleashing Your Personal Pride

You can unleash your personal pride by discovering your strengths and talents. Recognizing what makes you special is the first step in building your personal pride.

Envision a success story for your life. You need to chase realistic goals, such as doing well in your tests, learning new skills, and even working on your future career. When you achieve your goals, your personal pride will give you a significant boost.

You should own your uniqueness—whether it's a funky sense of style, a passion for something unusual, or a talent that makes you stand out. When you take pride in being authentically you, others will admire your confidence.

When things don't go as planned, view them as opportunities for growth. It's normal to make mistakes, and you should do your best to learn from them. Instead of dwelling on your setbacks, be proud of the lessons they've taught you. Resilience is an essential aspect of personal pride and will make you stronger for the next challenges you've got to deal with. You will always face challenges in your life; it's all about how you deal with them.

Celebrating your victories and achievements will help you gain more pride in them, even if you think they're not that important.

Use Your Voice

You shouldn't be afraid to use your voice and express your opinions. You can also use your voice to set boundaries and stand up against injustice. This can be difficult, especially if everyone's opinions and viewpoints are very different from your own, and you could have to face repercussions for your beliefs. In our current "cancel" culture, it could be difficult to express your true opinions and live as your authentic self.

Sadly, some people live their entire lives never using their voices. They think that once they're retired, they're not dependent on society much any longer; but for many, this moment never comes.

So, discover your strength and use your voice when you have the opportunity. We need people with the confidence and personal pride to use their voices to move society in the right direction. It's scary, but you'll be so proud of yourself when you're able to speak up.

If you use your voice and go against the status quo, you could potentially disrupt a negative social narrative and pave the way for a more authentic society. So, your willingness to stand up for what's right could help others to lead more meaningful lives.

Your voice is the strongest way in which you can rebel against the pressure to conform and embrace your unique personality. In the times we live in, we need to hear authentic voices, and if you express yourself, you can encourage people to think critically. You will be encouraging others to question, analyze, and form their own perspectives. Just imagine: By sharing your opinion, you can encourage independent thought and create a powerful ripple effect of independent thought. You can change the world! Remember, people who are powerful change-makers usually don't follow the crowd.

Speaking up also strengthens your resilience. The more you speak up when you encounter resistance and challenges, the more you'll strengthen your ability to deal with challenges, and you'll emerge even stronger.

When you use your voice authentically, especially when it goes against the status quo, you're building genuine connections. Others who share your convictions will be drawn to you, and you could form a supportive group of people who support your ideas.

Don't shy away from using your voice, especially when it goes against the status quo. Your dissenting opinions are the sparks that can introduce much-needed change in the world. The world urgently needs your unique perspective.

RESILIENCE AND YOUR PERSONAL PRIDE

Ever feel like life's tossing you into a whirlwind of challenges, dilemmas, and unexpected twists? Don't worry, your resilience and personal pride will get you through.

We've talked quite a bit about personal pride and how it can get you ahead in life, but what exactly is resilience?

Have you ever played an online game where your character faces relentless challenges, unexpected plot twists, and monsters at every turn? Well, guess what? Life's a bit like that, and that's where your resilience will get you ahead. It basically means that you can get back on your feet to continue if you get knocked down by challenges.

Resilience is like having a cheat code that helps you navigate through tough levels without giving up. You can turn setbacks into comebacks; you can hit "restart" after a tough day. You're simply capable of dealing with whatever life throws your way.

Think of yourself as playing one of your favorite online games. Every time you face a challenge, you not only survive but level up by gaining experience, new skills, and wisdom. Resilience is not about being invincible; it's about being the badass gamer who learns, grows, and becomes even more unstoppable at every level.

How can you learn resilience or gain more of it? It's something you should ideally learn in childhood— but don't worry, you're never too old to learn and can continue working on it throughout your life.

There are ways in which you can become better at resilience.

Building resilience is like sculpting a muscle—it demands consistent practice and dedication. Embracing challenges is the first step; instead of shying away, confront them as opportunities for personal growth. Develop a growth mindset that sees failures as learning experiences and focuses on improvement rather than performance.

Nurturing a support system is equally crucial. Forge connections with friends, family, or mentors; these social bonds provide a safety net during tough times. Sharpen your problem-solving skills by breaking down issues into manageable parts and working systematically toward solutions.

Don't neglect your well-being; it's the foundation of resilience. Prioritize sleep, maintain a balanced diet, and engage in regular exercise. Adversity is a powerful teacher, so reflect on challenging experiences, extracting valuable lessons for future reference. Embrace flexibility, adapt positively to change, and set realistic goals that build a sense of accomplishment with each achievement.

Mindfulness practices, like deep breathing or meditation, reduce stress and enhance present-moment awareness. Celebrate small wins—even minor accomplishments contribute to building a resilient mindset. Developing emotional intelligence is key to understanding and managing your emotions effectively.

And if the weight becomes too much to bear alone, seeking professional help is a sign of strength, not weakness. Remember, resilience is a journey, not a destination. Consistently integrating these practical strategies into your daily life will gradually fortify your resilience and empower you to navigate the challenges and uncertainties you'll still face in your life on your journey to adulthood.

The Advantages of Being Resilient

Resilience is about finding silver linings in life, learning from challenges, and understanding that setbacks are just plot twists in your grand adventure.

Personal pride is your emotional armor. It's not about being invincible; it's about acknowledging your vulnerabilities and still standing tall. When you take pride in who you are, you're arming yourself with self-love and acceptance—a shield against self-doubt.

Resilience isn't the absence of fear; it's the courage to face it. Whether it's the fear of failure, rejection, or the unknown, resilience empowers you to confront these fears head-on.

Resilience teaches you that every setback is a stepping stone to success. Personal pride reminds you that setbacks don't define you; your ability to rise and bounce back from them does. Personal pride encourages you to view mistakes not as failures but as opportunities for growth.

Resilience applauds your ability to celebrate victories, big or small. Personal pride is the cheerleader within, urging you to acknowledge your achievements. Whether it's acing a test, overcoming a fear, or simply getting through a tough day, your personal pride tells you that you deserve to celebrate yourself.

It's not just about the battles you win but the strength you exhibit. Resilience and personal pride are the foundations of that legacy. They're the stories you pass on, inspiring others to face challenges with courage and embrace their unique selves.

Self-Confidence and Personal Pride

Self-confidence is also an important aspect of personal pride. It can almost be described as a type of inner superpower.

It's about believing in your own abilities and the knowledge that you have what it takes to tackle whatever surprises life throws your way. As a teenager, your self-confidence will also help you discover your strengths and realize your potential.

Self-confidence encourages you to embrace your individuality. You'll realize that your talents, quirks, and interests make you a unique person.

Adolescence is a time of exploration and self-discovery, and self-confidence acts as your compass. It will help you go out into the unknown, discover new things, and then learn from your experience. Self-confidence will also help you see challenges as growth opportunities.

The journey to self-confidence involves overcoming self-doubt. It's about silencing your inner critic and realizing you're still confident, even when you make mistakes.

Personal pride is the armor formed from your self-confidence and self-love. You recognize your own worth and this enables you to live an authentic life. This also shields you from people's judgment and societal expectations.

Personal Pride and Cancel Culture

Personal pride instills self-respect. It teaches you to set healthy boundaries and helps you understand what you deserve in relationships and interactions. If you have pride in your values, you won't change them just for the sake of fitting in. This can be especially difficult in the time of cancel culture. Teenagers are still developing their identities, and it can be difficult to grow up in this environment.

Cancel culture could pressure you to conform to society's expectations, as you could fear the consequences of being canceled for standing up for something you believe in.

Personal pride, however, encourages you to live an authentic life. It's about staying true to your values, even when faced with external scrutiny. It's a buffer that fosters resilience. Cancel culture can be emotionally challenging, with public opinions influencing your sense of worth.

Cancel culture often blurs boundaries, with online and offline spheres intertwining. Personal pride empowers people to set healthy boundaries. It involves recognizing the difference between constructive criticism and unwarranted attacks, which allows you to protect your emotional and mental well-being.

Another big problem with cancel culture is that it stifles open dialogue and learning opportunities. However, your personal pride will encourage you to embrace a journey of lifelong learning and growth. It will allow you to be humble enough to listen and give you the courage to evolve. Your personal pride will encourage you to become a better version of yourself.

It also oversimplifies complex issues and is quick to point fingers at people, labeling them as good or bad. Your personal pride, however, will allow you to acknowledge the complexity of human experience.

Personal pride thrives in acknowledging the complexity of human experiences. It helps you avoid black-and-white thinking and realize that you have to make space for shades of gray in the human experience.

You can think about it in this way: Personal pride in the time of cancel culture is not about dismissing valid concerns or about being defiant; it's about being resilient in a way that you can withstand external social pressure, learn from your experience, and contribute in a positive way to society.

Self-confidence and personal pride complement each other. Self-confidence encourages you to try out new things, while personal pride encourages you to do so with self-respect and authenticity. Self-confidence will give you the power to be authentic.

PERSONAL PRIDE WORKSHEET

This worksheet is designed to help you explore and develop your personal pride. It focuses on important elements like self-confidence, resilience, and self-esteem.

Reflecting on Resilience

Have you had to deal with any challenging situations lately? How did you overcome them?

_____

_____

What strengths or qualities did you discover about yourself while you were dealing with these challenges?

_____

_____

How did you bounce back from setbacks, and what did you learn from the experience?

_____

_____

Embracing Your Authentic Self

List three things that make you unique and set you apart from others.

_____

_____

_____

How do you express your authentic self in different aspects of your life (school, friendships, hobbies)?

_____

_____

Share a moment when you felt most authentic. What were you doing, and how did it make you feel?

_____

_____

Building Self-Confidence

Write about an achievement, no matter how small, that boosted your confidence.

_____

_____

How do you handle self-doubt or criticism? List three positive affirmations you can tell yourself.

_____

_____

Set a realistic goal that will contribute to your self-confidence when you achieve it.

_____

_____

Nurturing Self-Esteem

Write down three things you appreciate about yourself, both internally (character traits) and externally (physical attributes).

_____

_____

_____

Reflect on a time when you felt proud of who you are. What made you feel this way?

_____

_____

How can you incorporate self-care practices into your routine to improve your well-being?

_____

_____

Turning Challenges Into Growth Opportunities

Write about a mistake you made. What lessons did you learn from it? What did you do to ensure that you don't make the same mistake again?

_____

_____

How can you turn setbacks into opportunities for personal growth?

_____

_____

What type of person do you want to become? Think about your strengths and the areas where you would need to improve.

_____

_____

Creating a Supportive Network

List three people (friends, family, mentors) who have made positive contributions to your life.

_____

_____

_____

How do you express your needs to your support network? Can they do anything to make you feel more supported?

_____

_____

Goal-Setting for Personal Growth

Set one short-term and one long-term goal related to your personal development.

_____

_____

Break down these goals into smaller, achievable steps.

_____

_____

_____

_____

KEY TAKEAWAYS

- Making your bed and maintaining a clean personal space contributes to self-respect, self-esteem, and personal pride.
- Personal pride acts as a shield against societal expectations, boosts your confidence, and helps you manage life's ups and downs.
- Personal pride deflects negative comments, making it difficult for bullies to affect your confidence.
- Sharing your experiences with your support network will help you become more resilient against bullies.
- Discover your strengths and uniqueness and celebrate your victories to boost your personal pride.
- Turn setbacks into opportunities for growth and learn from your mistakes to become more resilient.
- Expressing your opinions and going against the status quo builds personal pride and strengthens your resilience.
- Authentic voices disrupt negative social narratives, encouraging independent thought and positive change.

- Building resilience involves embracing challenges, developing a growth mindset, and maintaining a support system.
- Personal pride, as emotional armor, acknowledges vulnerabilities and encourages celebrating victories.
- Self-confidence is an inner superpower that encourages you to explore and embrace your individuality.
- Personal pride, formed from self-confidence and self-love, will protect you against judgment and societal expectations.
- In the time of cancel culture, personal pride encourages you to live authentically even if you're being scrutinized by others.

In Chapter 8, we're going to look at how emotional intelligence and emotional regulation can make your life easier.

CHAPTER 8
EMOTIONAL INTELLIGENCE, EMOTIONAL REGULATION, AND POSITIVE HABITS

Empathy and social skills are social intelligence, the interpersonal part of emotional intelligence. That's why they look alike.

DANIEL GOLEMAN

Emotional intelligence and the ability to regulate your emotions is crucial for your growth on your journey to adulthood. It sounds daunting, but it's simply about understanding and managing your emotions. It can make your teenage years a bit smoother, with fewer ups and downs.

Emotional intelligence has different parts: knowing yourself, controlling your reactions, understanding others, and staying motivated. Think about it as an emotional tool kit.

By now you know that life can be hectic at times for teenagers. Emotional intelligence and positive habits, even the simple ones like making your bed, will keep you on the right track and help you lead a calmer and more peaceful life.

WHY IS EMOTIONAL INTELLIGENCE IMPORTANT FOR TEENAGERS?

If you're emotionally intelligent, you'll understand not only what you're thinking and feeling, but you'll also have a greater understanding of the thoughts and feelings of others.

It has five key levels, and you can think of it almost as different stages of your favorite game:

1. Self-awareness: You know when you're happy, sad, excited, or whatever else you may be feeling, and you can also name these emotions. It's about recognizing your emotions and understanding why you feel the way you do.
2. Self-regulation: You're able to manage the emotions you've identified. This means you

don't just explode at people when you're angry with them; you walk away to cool down or you calm down before you approach someone to speak to them about a difficult issue.

3. Motivation: As we explained earlier in the book, motivation is the drive to achieve things and keep pushing forward. This could be anything from doing well on a test to excelling at a sport.

4. Empathy: This is like having a superpower to understand what others are feeling. It's not just seeing the world through your eyes; you can "walk in their shoes" to intimately experience what they're feeling.

5. Social skills: Imagine you're in a team-based game. Social skills are how well you work with others—communication, cooperation, and the rest. It's always handy to have good social skills, even if you feel that you're not a natural-born leader. Also, remember that if you're more introverted, you'll have different social needs from an extrovert. Leaving the party after two hours is okay, and you don't have to stay the entire night like your extroverted friend.

Now, why does emotional intelligence matter? High emotional intelligence means you're more likely to be able to handle challenges, build strong relationships, and make choices that lead to success.

Alexis Avoids Drama

Alexis wasn't your typical high school girl. While her friends often got caught up in high school drama, Alexis kept her distance from it, focused on her schoolwork and engaged in a healthy way with others.

Unlike many of her peers, she had the ability to navigate the difficult emotions that she experienced during her daily life, both at home and at school. Alexis not only recognized her own emotions, but she could also grasp what others were feeling.

One day, as the school was buzzing with excitement about an upcoming soccer match, Alexis found herself in the midst of a heated disagreement between her friends, Sarah and Jake. Alexis listened to both of them with as much empathy as she could muster.

Alexis eventually helped them see each other's point of view by using active listening and genuine understanding, They found that her input strengthened their relationship.

As the days passed, Alexis's reputation as the go-to person for emotional wisdom spread throughout the school. Students started asking her advice on everything from friendship troubles to exam stress. It wasn't just about recognizing emotions; it was about using that knowledge to make a positive impact.

One afternoon, she had to deal with a situation that challenged not only her emotional intelligence but also her ability to regulate her own emotions. The school was having an annual talent show, and there was a lot of tension as people clashed about which performance should take center stage.

When Alexis saw emotions were about to boil over, she gathered the representatives from the different groups and tried to get them to speak to each other. Finally, she got them not to only work together but to brainstorm a dazzling performance that used everyone's talents to their advantage.

The night of the talent show arrived, and the auditorium buzzed with anticipation. As the performance unfolded on stage, the audience applauded. It was a spectacular show, and everyone was impressed with Alexis's ability to get students to work together.

In the end, Alexis created a culture of understanding, cooperation, and resilience. She modeled emotional intelligence and emotional regulation to the other students, and they learned from her.

WHY DO YOU NEED TO BE ABLE TO REGULATE YOUR EMOTIONS?

Emotional regulation means you're able to manage and deal with your emotions in a socially acceptable way. You can recognize, understand, and effectively respond to various emotional experiences. Emotional regulation is an important part of emotional intelligence and is essential for your mental health and well-being.

When you're a teenager, the ability to regulate your emotions is especially important, for the following reasons:

You will experience significant hormonal changes and ongoing brain development during your teenage years. These changes can lead to heightened emotional experiences, and you could be emotionally volatile and irritable. For example, you might find yourself becoming annoyed by things and people who wouldn't normally annoy you. It can be an especially trying time for girls, who start getting their menstrual period and might experience emotional ups and downs as part of premenstrual syndrome (PMS). If you can learn emotional regulation skills during this time, it can help you deal with these changes more efficiently.

Everyone wants to feel socially accepted, and you might experience peer pressure. However, emotional regulation can help you deal with stress and emotions you could experience from social situations, and you will make healthier decisions and form more positive relationships.

Let's look at an example of good emotional regulation during a stressful situation at school:

Maya was a patient member of her school's school's debate club. Discussions often got heated and emotions ran high. One day, Maya found herself disagreeing with a fellow student named James.

Maya was becoming frustrated, and her initial instinct was to respond with a sharp retort. However, Maya took a deep breath, a technique that was always effective when it came to regulating her emotions. She realized that if she responded impulsively, the situation might only escalate further.

Maya excused herself from the debate momentarily, signaling to the moderator that she needed a moment to collect her thoughts. She went to the bathroom, drank some water, and focused on her breathing, which allowed her to put some distance between herself and the discussion.

After taking a few minutes to center herself, Maya returned to the debate with a composed demeanor. Instead of responding with aggression, she calmly articulated her perspective, using evidence and thoughtful reasoning to support her position. Maya also acknowledged the valid points James made, which demonstrated her empathy and her willingness to consider different viewpoints.

Maya's ability to step back, assess her emotional state, and respond thoughtfully contributed to a more constructive and respectful discussion.

Overwhelming Demands and Changes

You could be facing overwhelming academic pressures and challenges. Emotional regulation can help you to cope with this and to follow a balanced approach to your studies. For example, if you're feeling overwhelmed, it might be tempting to study all day and night for your exam and sleep and eat very little. You could stop exercising, as you could feel you just don't have the time. However, this is very unhealthy and will lead to burnout in the long term. You need a healthy study schedule that leaves you with time for the other important areas in your life.

Adolescence often brings significant life changes, such as transitioning to high school, facing new responsibilities, or dealing with changes in family structure. Emotional regulation skills can also help you better communicate with your family members. It's especially useful to have these skills if you need to deal with challenging people, for example, those who have personality disorders or other mental health challenges. If you're emotionally regulated, you can stay calm, even in difficult situations.

As a teenager, you're also still in the process of figuring out your identity. Emotional regulation can help you understand and accept your emotions, even the difficult ones, and this will assist you in forming a more stable sense of self.

Poor emotional regulation is linked to an increased likelihood of engaging in risky behaviors, such as substance abuse, self-harm, or impulsive decision-making. Developing emotional regulation skills reduces the risk of engaging in harmful activities, and it will be easier for you to make healthy choices.

EMOTIONAL INTELLIGENCE AND SOCIAL SKILLS

Emotional intelligence can help you with your social skills by helping you understand and navigate the emotions of others.

But before you can understand others, you need to be able to understand yourself.

Recognizing your own emotions is like having a road map to your inner world. It allows you to express yourself more clearly and understand why you react the way you do in different situations. This is the foundation of self-awareness.

Self-regulation is about being able to control your emotions. When you can control your emotions, especially the difficult ones like stress and frustration, it will help you have more successful social interactions. For example, you'll take responsibility and be accountable for the consequences of your actions, and you won't blame your friends if you do something wrong and end up being punished for it. If you get drunk at a social event and you're punished by your parents, it's a result of your decisions. If you're emotionally intelligent and able to self-regulate, you'll be able to accept that you have to deal with the consequences of what you did and understand that you can't place the blame on your friends.

Emotional intelligence also helps you step into your friends' shoes and understand what they're feeling and going through. This is empathy. For example, if your friend reacts in a certain way to something you've said or done, you'll be able to understand why they reacted the way they did.

This superpower will allow you to build connections and friendships that go beyond the surface, and you'll be able to create relationships with people who have different perspectives. After all, you want long-lasting relationships that add meaning to your life and aren't only superficial.

How does emotional intelligence tie in with your social skills? Effective communication becomes second nature when you're in tune with your emotions. You can express yourself clearly and listen actively, which reduces the chances that you will misunderstand others.

When you bring emotional intelligence to the table, it also becomes easier to manage conflicts. Your ability to approach conflicts calmly and rationally can help find solutions for everyone involved. You'll be the peacemaker in your social group, and you'll find that people will approach you to help them deal with their issues.

Working in groups also becomes easier. You become a collaborator who can adapt to different personalities, and you can navigate your way even through difficult group situations. This adaptability is an indicator of emotional intelligence and determines your success in social situations.

How to Be a Good Friend

Emotional intelligence and emotional regulation skills can help you to be a better friend. Trust is also one of the most important aspects of friendship. If you're reliable and keep your promises, you're creating a stronger foundation for lasting connections.

Being reliable and keeping promises fosters trust, creating a strong foundation for lasting connections. Being there for friends during challenging times and celebrating their successes will also help you strengthen friendship bonds.

On the more fun side, group activities and shared experiences can make you feel like you're one of the group and that you belong together. This doesn't just have to mean hanging out at the mall or going to the movies. Try to get out into the natural world with your friends and go on camping trips and hikes.

You should always be respectful of your friends' opinions. Understanding that people come from different backgrounds and that they have their own unique opinions will help you build a bigger and more diverse social network.

Avoid cliques and exclusivity. Include others and make an effort to be friends with a variety of different people.

Also, respect each other's boundaries. Understand that everyone needs space and that autonomy can contribute to a healthy and balanced friendship. Respecting boundaries helps prevent conflicts and ensures that friendships remain mutually beneficial.

Conflicts are a natural part of any relationship. You should learn to resolve conflicts in healthy ways, such as effective communication, compromise, and finding common ground. Successfully navigating conflicts strengthens friendships and teaches valuable problem-solving skills.

By mastering these qualities of a good friend, teenagers can contribute to the creation of a positive and supportive social network. These friendships not only provide emotional support but also play a crucial role in shaping the individuals they are becoming during this formative stage of life.

Being a good friend involves being a positive influence. You should encourage your friends to adopt healthy behavior and break their negative habits if they have any. You could also motivate each other to pursue your goals and make positive choices.

In the end, you need to be able to apologize and forgive your friends. We all make mistakes, and we need to be able to apologize.

Understand that everyone makes mistakes. If you're wrong, apologize sincerely. Similarly, be willing to forgive your friends and move past conflicts. Holding onto grudges can strain friendships.

Dealing With Peer Pressure

Respecting people's differences will also create an inclusive atmosphere where everyone feels valued and accepted. However, it's important that your friends also respect your opinion, and they shouldn't try to force you to have the same views as them.

It's difficult to deal with peer pressure and not give in to people with dominant personalities, but you need to develop this skill to live an authentic life and make the healthiest choices for you.

The main thing is you need to know your values. Understanding what's important to you makes it easier to make decisions that align with your principles, even when you have to deal with peer pressure.

You also need to learn to trust in your judgment and become confident about the choices you make. Confidence in your decisions makes it less likely that you'll be swayed by peer pressure. Stand firm in your beliefs, be proud of the choices you make, and believe in them.

It's also important to choose your friends wisely. Surround yourself with friends who respect your values and support your decisions. Their positive influence can help you stay true to yourself.

Assertiveness is important when it comes to resisting peer pressure. You need to learn to assert yourself without behaving aggressively. Be comfortable saying no when necessary and expressing your opinions respectfully. It's also important to have a plan for how to respond to peer pressure when you find yourself in this situation. This could involve having an excuse ready or knowing how to remove yourself from a challenging situation.

One of the ways of dealing with peer pressure is to be aware of what the consequences would be if you give in to it. You will need to think about how your choices can impact your well-being, goals, and relationships.

You should also educate yourself about the risks and consequences of negative behaviors like drinking or doing drugs. This will make it easier for you to resist negative consequences.

If you're struggling with this kind of pressure, you can also ask adults, such as your parents or teachers, for support. Talk to them about what you've experienced and the concerns you have. They can provide you with guidance.

Consider using humor to deal with the pressure you could be experiencing in social situations. A light-hearted response could always be good for deflecting pressure. Focusing on your goals could also help you deal with peer pressure. If you focus on your academic and sporting goals or your personal development, it can provide you with the motivation to deal with negative influences.

EMOTIONAL INTELLIGENCE AND REGULATION WORKSHEET

This worksheet will help you work on your emotional intelligence and regulation skills. Think carefully about the questions and be as honest as possible when you write down your answers.

Understanding Your Emotions

List Three Positive Emotions

_____

_____

_____

List Three Negative Emotions

_____

_____

_____

Describe a Situation for Each Emotion

Positive Emotion

_____

Negative Emotion

Identifying Emotions

Emotion Recognition

How do you feel when you receive a compliment? Do you feel happy, sad, or angry?

_____

_____

How do you feel when you have to deal with a difficult challenge? Do you feel confident, relaxed, anxious, or frustrated?

_____

_____

How do you feel when you spend time with your friends? Do you feel content, irritated, proud, or lonely?

_____

_____

Reflect on Personal Experiences

Write about a time when you identified and managed your emotions.

_____

_____

Emotional Regulation Strategies

Deep Breathing Exercise

Practice deep breathing for three minutes. Write down how you feel before and after.

_____

_____

Positive Self-Talk

Write down three positive affirmations to boost your mood and self-esteem.

_____

_____

Identify Triggers

List three situations or events that typically trigger negative emotions for you.

_____

_____

Emotional Regulation

What steps will you take when you're faced with a challenging emotion?

_____

_____

Reflect and Set Goals

Reflection

What have you learned about your emotions and regulation strategies? Did anything surprise you? What will you continue to work on?

_____

_____

Goals

Set one short-term and one long-term goal related to improving emotional intelligence and regulation.

Short-Term Goal:

_____

Long-Term Goal:

_____

KEY TAKEAWAYS

- Emotional intelligence and regulation are crucial for personal growth during your teenage years and will help you experience fewer ups and downs.
- Emotional intelligence involves knowing oneself, controlling reactions, understanding others, and staying motivated.
- High emotional intelligence allows understanding and managing one's emotions and the emotions of others and gives you the ability to deal with challenges more successfully.
- Emotional regulation is vital for teenagers due to hormonal changes, brain development, peer pressure, academic stress, and significant life changes during adolescence.
- Poor emotional regulation is linked to risky behaviors, while developing regulation skills reduces the likelihood of engaging in harmful activities.
- Being a good friend involves trust, positive influence, motivation, empathy, respect, inclusivity, and effective conflict resolution.

- Dealing with peer pressure requires knowing one's values, building confidence, choosing friends wisely, practicing assertiveness, having a plan, understanding consequences, and seeking support from trusted adults.

In Chapter 9, we will consider failure and success, and how these are influenced by procrastination.

CHAPTER 9
FAILURE, SUCCESS, PROCRASTINATION, AND A GROWTH MINDSET

Only those who dare to fail greatly can ever achieve greatly.

ROBERT F. KENNEDY

ccepting and dealing with failure is an important part of success. Challenges and setbacks are learning opportunities and can help you become more resilient. Failure teaches you valuable lessons that success often cannot. Often, it's a case that the more you fail, the more you learn. The successful people in the media and social media usually have a long list of failures behind them. We may think they have always been successful, but this is definitely not the case. If you delve deeper, you'll often find celebrity stories telling you how they achieved success through failure.

Failure can help you discover your strengths, weaknesses, and the areas where you need to improve. It builds character, instills perseverance, and helps you develop problem-solving skills. Always keep working on improving yourself. You should accept yourself where you are in your life at present but always strive to keep on improving and learning more in life.

Remember, each failure is an opportunity to prepare better for your future. So, you don't have to fear failure; it's part of your journey to become the best possible version of yourself.

EMBRACING FAILURE THROUGH A GROWTH MINDSET

As we've seen, you should never let current failures define your life and future. Redefining failure as a natural part of the learning process will empower you to approach obstacles with a positive mindset. It's simply encouraging you to learn more and to keep growing.

Learning and Adaptation

Failure is a natural part of any learning process. When we deal with setbacks, we have to analyze what went wrong, understand the underlying reasons, and then change our approach. We learn best through trial, error, and adaptation. So, if you mess up a presentation you have at school or don't do that well in an exam, don't beat yourself up about it or think that you're incapable of doing better. Learn what you can from the situation and work out how you can do better in the future. Remember that everyone has to learn, and no one started out knowing everything. Even the best athletes, writers, or artists were once babies and small children who didn't know anything and had to learn by making mistakes.

Growth Mindset and Lifelong Learning Mentality

If you have a growth mindset, you believe you can develop your skills and abilities through making an effort and learning from your experiences. It's also one of the key components of adopting a lifelong learning mentality. You're also more likely to take calculated risks, and it's a good mindset to have when you want to get ahead in life.

For example, if you dream of starting your own business, you need to take risks and deal with challenges and setbacks. People who can't deal with risk or don't believe they can learn and grow from their failures are usually more inclined to stay in "safe" jobs, where they are assured of receiving their salary every month. This is okay, too, but you can learn so much more and have more fun in life when you have a growth mindset.

If you believe you can develop your abilities, you're much more likely to step outside your comfort zone. You know that even if you fail initially, it will be a useful growth experience.

A growth mindset will also help you to think outside the box. Rather than only adhering to what is known and accepted, you can challenge norms and explore unconventional ideas. If you're willing to embrace unconventional thinking, you're likely a creative person with a growth mindset.

Creativity and a love for learning also go hand in hand and can motivate you to continue your learning journey and improve your creative talent, whether it's in the arts, writing, technology, or any other form of expression.

A growth mindset enables you to value persistent effort and continued hard work over the desire for instant success. You're passionate about what you do, and you're committed to continue learning in your field. For example, your dream is to become a successful published writer, but you realize that it can take many years to achieve that dream and you'll have to keep learning and practicing. You'll also be able to stay more relevant in the writing field if you continuously update your skills. So, for example, you take an SEO writing course that teaches you the skills you need for this type of writing.

What Is a Fixed Mindset?

We've talked a lot about a growth mindset, but to get a full understanding of this, you also know what a fixed mindset is.

You have a fixed mindset if you believe that your talents and abilities are fixed and you can't do anything to change them. People with a fixed mindset usually believe that they only have a certain amount of intelligence and talent that they can't change in any way throughout their lives.

People with this mindset often feel threatened by the success of others and tend to avoid challenges, as they want to appear competent at all costs. They often ignore constructive feedback and give up easily when they have to deal with challenges.

A fixed mindset can limit your growth as a person, and you could miss out on many exciting learning opportunities in your life.

Challenging the Norms

Fearless creative thinkers can venture into unconventional territories where they question established norms and keep an open mind to everything that's happening around them. This is a much-needed skill in our current society, in which certain undesirable and unhealthy behavior, such as manipulation, has become normalized.

Cultivate a mindset that values challenges, embraces mistakes, encourages continuous learning, supports adaptability, promotes open-mindedness, and inspires innovation. These are all skills needed to make meaningful contributions in a world where the current status quo needs to be challenged to create a better future.

As a lifelong learner, you'll be more inclined to approach information, ideas, and systems with curiosity, critical thinking, and a willingness to explore alternative perspectives. Your desire to challenge the status quo comes from a natural curiosity about how things work. You want to find more effective ways to do things. The world is dynamic, and what worked in the past may not work now or in the future. It's important to be flexible, open to change, and willing to explore new ideas.

PROCRASTINATION AND SUCCESS

Procrastination can stand in your way of achieving success. This is when you delay doing something until the last minute. For example, if you're not interested in the project you have to do for school, you keep putting it off until the night before you have to hand it in. You have to do a rush job then, and you can't do all the research you need to do, and the layout is a mess. So, what will the consequences be of this behavior? Well, you won't get a good grade, and you might even have to redo and resubmit your assignment. You'll have to deal with the same consequences if you only study the night before the exam.

If you behave this way, it's important to understand why, as this will be the only way you can change.

Perfectionism

Perfectionism is one reason for procrastination, and it can really kill your creativity. Perfectionism is often the result of the fear of failure. A fear of not meeting expectations or doing something perfectly can be paralyzing and lead to perfectionism, and you may

even avoid doing certain things. It could hold you
back from achieving.

Imagine you have a book you want to publish, but
you feel the need to keep making changes to it. You
used an editor, and some of your friends read it and
gave you feedback, which you incorporated.
However, you're still not satisfied, and you spend a
long time working on this book, just not getting it
done. Or, imagine you've created a beautiful painting, but you're just not happy with it, and you keep
adding layer upon layer of paint.

As a perfectionist, you might be setting unrealistically high standards for yourself, leading to chronic
stress and anxiety. Living with this fear can be overwhelming and cause you to live in a constant state of
stress.

The problem is that fear of failure can limit your
growth potential, and you can become stuck in your
development. We see this in some young people
struggling to adjust to adulthood and still relying on
their parents to run their lives for them well into their
20s. If your parents aren't encouraging you to get out
there and do things, you should try to surround
yourself with other supportive people and possibly
find a mentor who can help you get ahead.

Perfectionism can also affect your mental well-being and could encourage issues such as depression and eating disorders. Sadly, it can also influence your relationships with others and cause strained relationships, and you may find it difficult to form genuine relationships. Your friends may end up feeling that they're not good enough for you or that nothing they ever do pleases you.

The chronic stress associated with perfectionism can have physical consequences. You could struggle to sleep, suffer from headaches, and other health complaints.

Perfectionism can also lower your self-esteem and eventually could cause you to suffer from burnout. If you always chase perfection and don't look after yourself, it can eventually lead to mental and physical exhaustion.

Perfectionists usually struggle to enjoy their accomplishments, and they'll just move on to the next flaw or area they think should be improved.

If you struggle with perfectionism, you can achieve a more balanced approach to life. Work on cultivating self-compassion and accepting yourself with your imperfections.

Overcoming Perfectionism

So, how can you overcome perfectionism?

It involves adopting a more balanced and realistic mindset. One way is to set realistic goals that are achievable and break larger tasks into smaller, more manageable steps. These are the micro goals we discussed earlier in the book. This will reduce the pressure on you to be perfect.

As said before, we need to move our focus away from a perfect result to appreciating the effort we put into achieving something. Our learning and growth come from the attempt we put in, not the result; this can be empowering.

Another crucial step is to challenge our negative thoughts about ourselves. We need to be realistic in our expectations and acknowledge that nobody is perfect.

Setting time limits for your tasks and school projects can also help you prevent overthinking and perfectionism. If you know something has to be done by a certain time, it creates a sense of urgency. You need to complete something to be good enough, rather than perfect, which is impossible. For example, writers and editors know that it's impossible to produce an absolutely perfect text. There will always be a comma or full stop somewhere that can be moved, but hardly anyone will recognize these small imperfections.

It's important to understand the difference between high standards and reaching for perfection. Perfection is unrealistic, but it's perfectly acceptable to set high standards for yourself. Try to get constructive criticism or feedback on the work you've done, and then empower yourself by improving on this. Just remember not to take criticism personally but to use it as an opportunity for growth.

Procrastination

One common cause of procrastination is the conflict between instant gratification and long-term goals. It's so much easier to prioritize activities that will give you immediate pleasure, such as going to the movies with your friends or spending time on social media. Tasks with long-term benefits, like homework and studying, just may not seem that interesting.

Overcoming Procrastination

It's important to set long-term goals for yourself that you know are going to take a long time to achieve and that you may not find all that interesting.

Specific, measurable objectives can give you a sense of direction and purpose. Connecting the task to your personal goals, values, or interests adds relevance, making it more meaningful and engaging. Also, break down your tasks into smaller ones to make them less overwhelming.

When it comes to completing these tasks you don't enjoy all that much, you can also motivate yourself when you reach your milestones.

When it's hard to motivate yourself to keep going, visualize the satisfaction you'll feel after completing the task. Try to somehow connect the tasks to your interests to make them more enjoyable. For example, if you have to write a long essay for your English class, try to select a topic that interests you and on which you won't mind doing research.

Consider changing your environment to refresh your perspective. For example, could you work on your tasks outside in your garden or sit in another room? Also, get up regularly and walk around, as it's impossible to focus for hours on end.

Recognizing the intrinsic value of the task—how it contributes to personal or intellectual growth—can also boost your motivation. For example, if you had to do a lot of research for a history assignment, what would you take away from it? Is there important information that you can use for writing your own blog?

Leveraging technology wisely, such as using educational apps or gamified learning platforms, can introduce an element of fun to tasks that would otherwise cause you to procrastinate.

Gamified learning is like turning your studies into a fun game. Instead of just reading or answering questions, you earn points, badges, and rewards for doing well. It's a way to make learning more enjoyable by adding elements of games, like levels to complete, challenges to overcome, and even friendly competition with your friends and classmates.

The best option is to experiment with different approaches. By applying these strategies, you can transform tasks with long-term benefits into more interesting and engaging activities and you'll be less likely to procrastinate.

The Difference Between Max's and Lily's Mindsets

Max and Lily were two friends preparing for their school's general knowledge competition and quest.

Max had always been smart and confident, as he effortlessly aced tests and was able to understand new concepts with very little effort. Lily was persistent, and she worked very hard, but she didn't think she was as smart as Max.

As the competition approached, Max and Lily decided to study together. Max had a fixed mindset and believed that his intelligence was a fixed trait. He wanted to maintain the perception that he was the smartest in town. He avoided challenging topics and only focused on what he already knew. Max didn't think he could excel in areas that were unfamiliar to him.

Lily, with her growth mindset, saw the competition as an opportunity to learn and grow. She embraced challenging subjects, knowing that the more she learned, the better equipped she would be for the future. She didn't fear failing, as she knew it would help her do better in future competitions.

As they studied, Max often chose tasks he was already good at, while Lily chose more complicated subjects where she would have to make an effort. Max became frustrated and discouraged when they had to deal with difficult subjects.

Lily was more enthusiastic. She asked questions, sought help, and persisted through the difficulties. She realized that while she didn't understand everything, she would be able to figure it out.

When the day of the competition arrived, the questions covered a broad range of topics, including the challenging quantum physics section. Max hesitated on many of the questions, as he was scared that he would get them wrong. Lily was determined and put a lot of effort into every question she received, as she wanted to learn as much as possible.

Lily performed exceptionally well, not just because of her natural abilities but because of her attitude toward challenges and failure. Max, however, struggled with the questions and ended up not doing well at all.

As the results were announced, Max learned a valuable lesson from Lily. He discovered that embracing a growth mindset, being open to challenges, and seeing failures as opportunities to learn were the real keys to success.

Max and Lily remained friends, and they were committed to fostering a growth mindset and supporting each other in their quest for knowledge.

FAMOUS FAILURES—WELL-KNOWN PEOPLE WHO ACHIEVED SUCCESS AFTER SEVERAL FAILURES

Most of us enjoy reading about successful celebrities and what they have achieved in their lives. However, did you know that many of them were huge failures before they achieved success? Let's take a look at some of them.

Stephen King

Stephen King is arguably one of the greatest living writers. He has written more than 60 novels of considerable length. Even in his 70s, his new releases consistently make it onto the bestseller list.

However, his journey to the top wasn't simple or easy. He started writing in his teenage years, and he accumulated a large collection of rejection letters. He eventually started writing his first novel, *Carrie*, when he was working as a teacher in rural Maine. He got his first true taste of success when *Carrie* became popular.

Even *Carrie* had been rejected more than 30 times. He initially discarded the manuscript after receiving another rejection, but his wife rescued the manuscript and encouraged him to try again. Today, he has left a significant mark on the literary landscape.

J.K. Rowling

J.K. Rowling serves as a testament to the idea that anyone can be successful at any time of their lives.

Rowling always wanted to be a writer, but life placed many challenges in her way. She struggled with depression after her mother's death. Her first marriage fell apart, and she struggled with the difficult role of being a single mother.

Battling against the constraints of welfare, Rowling found herself in the complex juggling act of providing for her child, pursuing an education, and attempting to carve out the time to write a novel, among all her other responsibilities.

Rowling admits she saw herself as a failure, initially, but she also attributes her eventual success to her sense of feeling like a failure. Before *Harry Potter* captivated audiences worldwide, Rowling was a divorced mother grappling with the challenges of welfare, navigating the demands of education, and trying to find the time to write her first novel in the little time she had left.

George Lucas

George Lucas is a cinematic icon, with his *Star Wars* movies ranking among the most lucrative franchises in Hollywood history. Since the release of the first film, *Star Wars: A New Hope* in 1977, the movies have consistently dominated the box office.

However, the journey of *Star Wars* to the grandeur of the big screen wasn't an easy one. Most of the major studios first turned down the opportunity to work on this project.

Fox finally took the gamble, inspired by the hope that *Star Wars* would follow in the footsteps of *American Graffiti*, one of George Lucas's earlier successful movies.

During the filming of *Star Wars*, Lucas's approach wasn't understood by all involved. Tensions simmered between him, the actors, the crew, and the studio executives. Fox also struggled to find an innovative way to market the movie.

Despite the challenges, *Star Wars* became a hit soon after it was released. The *Star Wars* franchise burgeoned into a billion-dollar industry and established itself as a cultural phenomenon.

Walt Disney

Even visionary creator Walt Disney had to walk a tough road to success.

At the age of 22, Disney found himself employed at a newspaper firm in Missouri, only to face an unexpected termination. The newspaper editor didn't think he was creative enough for the job.

However, Disney overcame this critique by achieving monumental success. His animated films, which featured characters like Mickey and Minnie Mouse and Daffy Duck, earned him over 30 Academy Awards. This triumph showed he definitely didn't have a deficit when it came to creativity.

Madonna

Madonna is an icon who is known for pushing the boundaries. Today, she is one of the most influential and top-selling female musicians in history. Yet, the path to her fame was littered with challenges.

Dance was her escape from a childhood in which she had to care for seven younger siblings. She eventually decided to leave college and ventured into the competitive world of professional dance in New York City.

Her initial years in New York were very difficult. She became a victim of crime when she was held at gunpoint and sexually assaulted. Her apartment was burgled three times. Despite these hardships, she persevered in her dance career, sustaining herself through waitressing and modeling nude for art classes.

Madonna's resilience got her through the difficult times and eventually led to success. Finally, in 1982, her single "Holiday" secured a spot in the Billboard Top 20, and that was the turning point for her career.

Eminem

Marshall Bruce Mathers III, who became known as Eminem, achieved widespread acclaim for his song "Lose Yourself," earning accolades, including the Academy Award for Best Original Song and the Grammy for Best Rap Song.

However, Eminem's journey was full of challenges, and he almost died more than once.

He grew up in poor neighborhoods where he was an outsider and got beaten up regularly. He failed the eighth grade three times before finally dropping out of school. Marshall later admitted that it happened because he was never in school and had to hold down more than one job from a young age to help his family survive.

Eminem's true passion lay in rap, a pursuit he began at the age of 14. By 17, he had established himself in the hip-hop community. However, being a white rapper posed a unique challenge, and it took him some time to prove his success during rap battles.

The turning point in Eminem's career came when Dr. Dre discovered his talent, provided him with mentorship, and secured him a recording contract. Today, Eminem is regarded as one of the most successful and influential figures in the history of rap.

WORKSHEET: NAVIGATING FAILURE, SUCCESS, AND PROCRASTINATION AND FOSTERING A GROWTH MINDSET

Section 1: Understanding Failure

Reflect on Failure

Think about a time when you had to deal with failure and you didn't achieve the outcome you wanted. What happened? How did it make you feel? How did you deal with it?

_____

_____

Changing Perspective

Think about different ways in which you can view failure. Do you have the ability to see a setback as a learning opportunity? Write down one lesson or insight you gained from a past failure.

_____

_____

Resilience Building

List three ways you can build resilience to bounce back from failures. This can be anything from looking for support to setting smaller goals for yourself.

_____

_____

_____

Section 2: Embracing Success

Defining Success

Write down your definition of success. Think about your short-term and long-term goals.

_____

_____

Success Stories

Write about a time when you were successful. What did you do to achieve success, and how did it make you feel?

_____

_____

Setting Achievable Goals

Identify one short-term and one long-term goal. Break them down into smaller steps to make them more achievable.

_____

_____

_____

_____

Section 3: Tackling Procrastination

Recognizing Procrastination

What do you usually procrastinate? Why do you think you delay these tasks?

_____

_____

Procrastination Triggers

Write about situations or feelings that cause you to procrastinate. How can you address or overcome these triggers?

_____

_____

Creating a Proactive Plan

Write a plan to tackle procrastination. Include specific strategies like setting deadlines or breaking down tasks or goals into smaller parts. Continue writing in your journal if the space below is not enough.

_____

_____

_____

_____

Section 4: Fostering a Growth Mindset

Understanding Growth Mindset

Describe what a growth mindset means to you. How is it different from a fixed mindset?

_____

_____

Applying Growth Mindset

Do you have any challenges you need to deal with at the moment? How can you use a growth mindset to deal with these challenges? List at least three ways you can view the challenges as opportunities.

What have you learned from this worksheet? How can these insights help you deal with failure, success, and procrastination, and develop a growth mindset moving forward?

KEY TAKEAWAYS

- Challenges and setbacks are opportunities for learning and growth. You will often only experience success after several failures. Most people who are successful and well-known today had to go through this process.

- Failure will help you identify strengths, weaknesses, and areas for improvement. It builds character, instills perseverance, and will improve your problem-solving skills.

- Fear of failure can lead to perfectionism, and you could set unrealistically high standards for yourself. Perfectionism could limit your creativity, cause chronic stress, and stifle personal development.

- Overcoming perfectionism involves setting realistic goals, appreciating effort over perfect results, and challenging negative thoughts.

- You should see constructive criticism as a growth opportunity.

- Procrastination often arises from prioritizing immediate pleasure over long-term goals.

- Setting specific, measurable goals; breaking tasks into smaller steps; and finding intrinsic value in the task can combat procrastination.

In Chapter 10, we're going to look at how critical thinking skills can help you tackle life.

CHAPTER 10
CRITICAL THINKING SKILLS

> *Critical thinking is the ability to think clearly and rationally, understanding the logical connection between ideas. It's about being active (as opposed to reactive) in your learning and questioning everything until you're satisfied you understand the whole picture.*

ROBERT H. ENNIS

Shaun, Stacy, and Chris were friends who lived in a society where questioning, analyzing, and challenging ideas could get them into trouble. The education system prioritized rote memorization over independent thought, and misinformation spread like wildfire. The expectation was that everyone should always comply with the status quo.

The friends were beginning to notice cracks in this system. While their classmates accepted information without questioning everything, and decisions were made based on tradition instead of reason, the three friends felt rebellious, and they wanted something more.

One day in history class, the teacher provided them with information that didn't make sense to Shaun. Instead of blindly accepting what he heard, Shaun raised his hand and asked his teacher a critical question. The teacher wasn't used to being challenged and struggled to answer the question. The classroom was silent.

Shaun and his friends decided to form a small group that dedicated themselves to improving their critical thinking skills. They shared books and ideas that encouraged questioning and analysis. As they delved deeper, they discovered the power of discernment and the ability to see beyond the surface of information.

The group grew, and teenagers started questioning the world around them. The society that once discouraged independent thought began to witness a subtle revolution led by young people with critical thinking skills They organized debates, started a school newspaper that challenged the official narrative, and even convinced some teachers to incorporate critical thinking into their lessons.

The change was gradual but transformative. The once-passive society began to realize the importance of questioning, analyzing, and challenging ideas. With critical thinking as their guiding light, the teenagers not only changed their world but also set an example for future generations.

WHAT IS CRITICAL THINKING?

Critical thinking is your ability to analyze information, understand the logical connections between ideas, and make informed decisions. Critical thinkers don't just accept everything at face value. They ask questions, think independently, and evaluate evidence.

If you want to be a critical thinker, you must be open-minded and ready to explore different perspectives. Critical thinking will help you navigate your life with a clear mind.

What happens when people in a society don't have critical thinking skills? You may think critical thinking sounds abstract, but it's an essential skill for the normal functioning of a society. If too many people don't have this skill, things can go wrong.

First, misinformation and propaganda become more prevalent, as people aren't able to question and verify the information they receive. This can lead to the spread of false narratives, and even history can be changed to a version of the truth that those in charge prefer. This is becoming easier in a time where the creation of deepfakes and false information has become easy.

A deepfake is like a tricky digital video or audio trick made with super-smart computer programs. These programs change regular videos, making it seem like people are saying or doing things they never really did. They can look very real, making it hard to tell what's true and what's not. It can be difficult to identify these deepfakes, but it's possible by using your critical thinking skills.

Look at facial expressions and movements when you're watching a video. Deepfakes often struggle to replicate natural features, so look for inconsistencies like unnatural blinking or awkward expressions. Check the synchronization of lips and speech, as deepfakes often don't get these right. Also, evaluate the audio quality for distortions, pauses, or discrepancies between the speaker's voice and the message. There can also be inconsistencies in the lighting and shadows used in videos.

Decision-Making Suffers

If people don't have critical thinking skills, decision-making at individual and societal levels may suffer. If you can't think critically, your decisions will be based on emotions, biases, or incomplete information rather than a thorough analysis of the situation. This could have a negative effect on your school career and your relationships.

It becomes easier to manipulate people if they're incapable of critical thinking. A society that lacks critical thinking may lack innovation and progress. Critical thinkers are more likely to question existing norms and explore new ideas, which will lead to creativity and advancement in different fields.

That's why you need to learn critical thinking from a young age. A society without critical thinkers will eventually experience a weakening of its democracy and a lack of intellectual growth. It will become more susceptible to misinformation and manipulation.

A Valuable Habit for Teenagers

So, why is critical thinking a valuable habit for you as a teenager specifically?

First, it will empower you to be able to analyze information independently. In a world filled with diverse perspectives and information sources, critical thinking will help you evaluate information and make informed decisions.

Second, critical thinking fosters creativity. It will encourage you to explore alternatives, question assumptions, and think outside the box and will help you build a mindset that is geared toward innovation and problem-solving.

Moreover, critical thinking will prepare you for the complexities of the knowledge economy. It equips you with the ability to navigate challenges, adapt to change, and make good judgments. This skill will become increasingly important when you become an adult, as you will encounter diverse opinions and face ethical dilemmas, and you'll need to make decisions that could have a serious impact on your life.

Critical thinking also enhances communication skills. If you can think critically, you'll be better equipped to articulate your thoughts, express your ideas coherently, and engage in constructive dialogue. This skill is important for your academic success, interpersonal relationships, and future career.

Lastly, critical thinking cultivates a sense of responsibility. It helps you take ownership of your decisions and helps you become aware of the consequences of your choices. You'll also be better at considering the ethical implications of your choices.

Critical Thinking Can Help You With Problem-Solving

You need problem-solving skills to lead a successful life and get ahead in life. Critical thinking is the key to this process, as it can help you with finding creative solutions and making informed decisions.

Critical thinking can help you solve problems in the following ways:

- It can help you identify the central problems or issues within a complex situation. It helps you see that the problem can be broken down into its essential components to understand the nature of the challenge.
- It helps you gather and evaluate relevant information before jumping to conclusions. Analyze data, consider multiple perspectives,

and assess the reliability of sources before you come to a conclusion about the problem.

- Critical thinking helps you question assumptions, both your own and others. This will ensure that your problem-solving approach is based on sound reasoning.

- This way of thinking lets you explore different possibilities and consider unconventional approaches. This will increase the likelihood that you'll find innovative answers to your problems.

- Critical thinking helps you make decisions by weighing the pros and cons of situations. It helps you anticipate potential outcomes as well as the risks and benefits associated with each decision.

- If you're a critical thinker, you can articulate your thoughts clearly and concisely. This skill is vital when it comes to conveying the nature of a problem, discussing potential solutions with others, and gaining support for the chosen course of action.

- Critical thinking can help you improve continuously. After implementing a solution, critical thinkers assess the results, learn from the experience, and use this knowledge to enhance their problem-solving skills in the future.

- Critical thinking gives you the tools and mindset necessary to approach problems systematically, make informed decisions, and adapt to various challenges effectively.

Dealing With Social Media and Social Contagion

Social media has become one of the best ways to keep in touch with family and friends who don't live close to you. However, it can also act as an agent for social contagion, which means it can spread attitudes and beliefs through a group of people that then influences others and creates a domino effect. It's almost like spreading an infectious disease. The people who receive this information then adopt similar attitudes, behaviors, and even emotional states.

Peer pressure and the desire for social conformity can also play a role in social contagion. Examples include the spreading of rumors and the emergence of collective behaviors and emotions.

Social media can cause social contagion in the following ways:

- It allows information to be shared instantly with a wide audience. Ideas can spread very fast and influence a large number of people. People then tend to imitate this viral content.

- Social media algorithms often create echo chambers where you are exposed only to content that aligns with your existing beliefs and opinions. This could spread certain ideologies and contribute to the polarization of attitudes within specific online communities.

- It can also facilitate the spread of emotions. When users share emotional content, whether positive or negative, it can influence the emotional states of others who come across that content. This can affect the collective mood of online communities.

Critical thinking can protect you from becoming a victim of social contagion or mass hysteria.

Critical thinking can help you approach information more independently and will help you consider different perspectives, as well as the available evidence. You will become more aware of the potential for misinformation, manipulation, or propaganda. It will be easier not to adopt beliefs or behaviors because they're popular.

When it comes to making decisions, critical thinkers prioritize evidence over emotional and social influences. They're less likely to be swayed by emotions or opinions and are less likely to use logical reasoning.

Finally, critical thinking will limit the influence of social media on your life.

A Short Checklist For Critical Thinking

If you can tick the following steps, you're on the right course when it comes to critical thinking:

- Do you understand the challenge that needs to be resolved?
- Have you gathered information from diverse sources before making your decision?
- Do you have certain biases and assumptions? Have you challenged them before making a decision?
- Have you assessed the reliability of your information before making your decision?
- Do you have multiple potential solutions for a complex problem?
- Have you reflected on your solution and if it was effective?

WORKSHEET—CRITICAL THINKING SKILLS

This worksheet will help you develop critical thinking skills by applying them to everyday scenarios.

Scenario 1: Making Decisions

You're going out with your friends for the weekend, but you have a limited budget. You can go to the movies, try a new restaurant, or hang out at the park or somebody's house.

Think about what the best option will be by considering factors like time, cost, and everyone's preferences.

Gather information about each option and list them.

_____

_____

_____

_____

Evaluate the pros and cons and consider the outcomes and consequences.

_____

_____

_____

_____

Make your decision and explain why you made that choice.

_____

_____

_____

_____

Scenario 2: Problem-Solving

You and your classmates are working on a group project. You disagree about which approach you should be following. Use critical thinking to solve this conflict.

Write down the issue that's causing the conflict below.

_____

_____

_____

_____

Allow each group member to give their perspective and write it down below.

_____

_____

_____

_____

Brainstorm solutions to the problem and write them down below.

_____

_____

_____

_____

Scenario 3: Social Media Dilemma

You find a post on social media that's sharing information you don't agree with. Some of your friends have shared it. Apply critical thinking to decide if you should share it as well.

Did reliable sources share this information?

_____

_____

_____

_____

Research the claims made in the post. Are there credible sources supporting or contradicting the information?

_____

_____

_____

_____

Based on your evaluation, will you share the post? Explain your decision.

_____

_____

_____

_____

KEY TAKEAWAYS

- Critical thinking can help you when it comes to analyzing information, understanding logical connections, and making informed decisions.

- Critical thinking involves questioning, independent thinking, and evaluating evidence.
- Society needs critical thinkers to be able to function in a normal way.
- If a society is incapable of critical thinking, misinformation, propaganda, and manipulation can become widespread.
- It's easier to manipulate people if they're incapable of critical thinking.
- Critical thinking prepares you for the complexities of the knowledge economy and ethical decision-making.
- Social media can encourage social contagion by spreading certain attitudes and beliefs. You're less likely to fall prey to this if you're good at critical thinking.
- Critical thinking protects against misinformation, manipulation, and social conformity.

CONCLUSION

It's possible to navigate your turbulent teenage years with pride and resilience. We're coming to the end of our journey together, and we want to summarize exactly how you can do this.

Let's look at some of the key ideas and takeaways in this book.

KEY IDEAS AND TAKEAWAYS

We started this book with the revelation that a simple act such as making your bed, could become an important anchor in your personal development journey.

A clean and organized personal space becomes a symbol of self-respect and establishes the foundation for positive habits that contribute to your mental well-being.

We considered how you can use personal pride as a form of protection to get you through your difficult teenage years, especially by protecting you against the judgment of others. Personal pride is instrumental in deflecting societal expectations and will help you become more resilient in dealing with whatever life sends your way.

The book provides you with guidelines for developing personal pride, recognizing your strengths, embracing authenticity, and celebrating the victories in your life. We reframed failures as opportunities for growth. They foster resilience, an indispensable companion on the journey to adulthood.

We also looked at some scary but inspiring stuff, such as the power of using your voice authentically even when it goes against the status quo. In an era marked by cancel culture, personal pride is an all-important force that encourages authenticity, resilience, and the courage to deal with society's pressures in a respectful way.

We laid bare the advantages of resilience and the important role it plays in enabling you to confront your fears, viewing setbacks as stepping stones and celebrating victories—big or small. Your personal pride is your emotional armor which also protects you against self-doubt.

Self-confidence emerged as a complementary force to personal pride, an inner superpower that can guide you on your journey to self-awareness.

Even in the era of cancel culture, where societal expectations can be overwhelming, personal pride stands firm against the dangers of conformity. It encourages us to live authentically and set healthy boundaries and also encourages open dialogue and learning opportunities.

Emotional intelligence emerges as a crucial force, helping you confront your fears, view setbacks as growth opportunities, and celebrate victories.

Self-confidence, a companion to personal pride, is your superpower and helps you face challenges with a positive outlook.

We reframed setbacks as stepping stones for growth, emphasizing the importance of resilience and the courage to face challenges head-on.

We also looked at critical thinking as a crucial skill that can help you analyze information, question assumptions, and make informed decisions. It acts as a shield against misinformation and societal manipulation, encouraging independent thought and a nuanced approach to challenges.

Integrating Making Your Bed and Other Good Habits

It all starts with the simple act of making your bed. The seemingly simple act of making your bed, as explored earlier, transcends mere tidiness. It becomes a ritual of self-respect and an affirmation that you deserve to inhabit a clean and organized space. Good habits intertwine with our daily routines and contribute to our mental well-being.

The act of making your bed goes beyond self-respect; it also shows that you respect shared spaces. A tidy room is not just a personal sanctuary but a testament to valuing the shared environment, especially if you and your friends or siblings spend a lot of time there.

Call to Action: Apply Your Personal Pride Symphony

As we come to the end of our enriching journey, we remind you to apply the harmonies of personal pride and resilience in your life. We encourage you to use your voice, embrace challenges, and celebrate victories.

Share your story, stand tall against negativity, and be authentic. Remember, the symphony of your life is uniquely yours.

Set realistic goals, embrace your uniqueness, and face challenges with resilience and personal pride. Your journey is a symphony in the making, and every note will contribute to the legacy of strength you're building.

REFERENCES

Clear, J. (2015, June 28). *5 useful reminders for when you want to give up.* James Clear. https://jamesclear.com/giving-up

Clear, J. (2016, June 28) *The Goldilocks rule: How to stay motivated in life and business.* James Clear. https://jamesclear.com/goldilocks-rule

Clear, J. (n.d.). *Habit stacking: How to build new habits by taking advantage of old ones.* James Clear. https://jamesclear.com/habit-stacking

Daniel Goleman quotes. (2019). BrainyQuote. https://www.brainyquote.com/authors/daniel-goleman-quotes

Edmondson, A. (2011). *Strategies for learning from failure.* Harvard Business Review. https://hbr.org/2011/04/strategies-for-learning-from-failure

Emotional intelligence. (n.d.). Psychology Today. https://www.psychologytoday.com/za/basics/emotional-intelligence

Getting started with mindfulness. (2018). Mindful. https://www.mindful.org/meditation/mindfulness-getting-started

Gratitude journal. (2018). Greater Good Science Center. https://ggia.berkeley.edu/practice/gratitude_journal

Hage, J. (2021, March 24). *25 insightful quotes about decluttering the mind.* Filling the Jars. https://www.fillingthejars.com/quotes-about-decluttering-the-mind

Hurley, K. (2022, July 14). *What is resilience?* Everyday Health. https://www.everydayhealth.com/wellness/resilience

Lawler, M. (2023, March 17). *What is self-care and why is it critical for your health?* Everyday Health. https://www.everydayhealth.com/self-care

Locker, M. (n.d.). *8 easy ways to start decluttering your home.* AARP.

https://www.aarp.org/home-family/your-home/info-
2021/simple-decluttering-and-organization-tips.html

Marinoff, Evelyn. (2019, July 8). *Why is internal motivation so
powerful (and how to find it).* Lifehack. https://www.lifehack-
.org/839224/internal-motivation

Maxwell, M. A. (n.d.). *Council post: Why failing is an important part
of success.* Forbes. https://www.forbes.com/sites/forbesbusi-
nesscouncil/2022/07/18/why-failing-is-an-important-part-of-
success/?sh=4dce449f4d62

Miles, M. (2022, March 30). *Why learning from failure is your key to
success.* BetterUp. https://www.betterup.com/blog/learning-
from-failure

Parent Self Care. (n.d.). *10 ways to care for our bodies and living space
during a quarantine.* Parent Self Care. https://parentselfcare.-
com/blog/10-ways-to-care-for-our-bodies-and-living-space-
during-a-quarantine

Scott, E. (2020). *5 self-care practices for every area of your life.* Verywell
Mind. https://www.verywellmind.com/self-care-strategies-
overall-stress-reduction-3144729

Scott, S. J. (2023, September 12). *Famous failures: 30 stories of
successful people who once failed.* Develop Good Habits.
https://www.developgoodhabits.com/successful-people-
failed

Segal, J., et al. (2023, February 28). *Improving emotional intelligence
(EQ).* HelpGuide. https://www.helpguide.org/articles/men-
tal-health/emotional-intelligence-eq.htm

Simple tips to make decluttering your home a breeze. (n.d.) School-
house. https://www.schoolhouse.com/blogs/how-to/our-top-
tips-for-decluttering-your-home?gad_source=1&gclid=CjwK-
CAiAmZGrBhAnEiwAo9qHiVPT-rulkjQIKcpxE-gF4uS-
8Lzc6MeHp0fBNUVnfPvX4QfhJzJh5BoCiz8QAvD_BwE

Sutton, J. (2019, January 3). *What is resilience and why is it important
to bounce back?* PositivePsychology. https://positivepsycholo-
gy.com/what-is-resilience

The power of intrinsic motivation. (2021, January, 5). Psychology Today. https://www.psychologytoday.com/us/blog/mind-brain-and-value/202101/the-power-intrinsic-motivation

31 quotes to inspire good habits. (n.d.). Productive and Free. https://www.productiveandfree.com/blog/31-habit-quotes

Walker, S. (2019, March 2). *Bed this down.* Newcastle Herald. https://www.newcastleherald.com.au/story/5930302/bed-this-down

Walsh, K. (2023, February 13). *What is habit stacking — and why it helps with behavior change.* EverydayHealth. https://www.everydayhealth.com/emotional-health/habit-stacking-and-why-it-might-help-your-behavior-changes-stick